101 Chess Opening Surprises

Graham Burgess

First published in the UK by Gambit Publications Ltd 1998

A copy of the British Library Cataloguing in Publication data is available from the British Library

ISBN 1 901983 02 1

DISTRIBUTION:
Worldwide (except USA): Biblios Distribution Services, Star Rd, Partridge Green, West Sussex, RH13 8LD, England.
USA: BHB International, Inc, 994 Riverview Drive, Totowa, New Jersey 07511, USA.

For all other enquiries (including a full list of all Gambit Chess titles) please contact the publishers, Gambit Publications Ltd, 69 Masbro Rd, Kensington, London W14 0LS.
Fax +44 (0)171 371 1477. E-mail 100561.3121@compuserve.com.

Edited by Graham Burgess
Typeset by Petra Nunn
Printed in Great Britain by Redwood Books, Trowbridge, Wilts.

10 9 8 7 6 5 4 3 2 1

Gambit Publications Ltd
Managing Director: GM Murray Chandler
Chess Director: GM John Nunn
Editorial Director: FM Graham Burgess
Assistant Editor: GM John Emms
German Editor: WFM Petra Nunn

Contents

Symbols

+	check
++	double check
#	checkmate
!!	brilliant move
!	good move
!?	interesting move
?!	dubious move
?	bad move
??	blunder
+–	White is winning
±	White is much better
⩲	White is slightly better
=	equal position
∓	Black is slightly better
∓	Black is much better
–+	Black is winning
Ch	championship
Cht	team championship
Wch	world championship
Ct	candidates event
IZ	interzonal event
Z	zonal event
OL	olympiad
jr	junior event
wom	women's event
mem	memorial event
rpd	rapidplay game
corr	correspondence game
1-0	the game ends in a win for White
½-½	the game ends in a draw
0-1	the game ends in a win for Black
(n)	nth match game
(11a)	see diagram 11a (etc.)
W (top of page)	an idea for White
B (top of page)	an idea for Black
W (by diagram)	White to play
B (by diagram)	Black to play

Introduction

Surprise is an extremely powerful weapon in chess and especially in the opening. A player who is surprised in the opening will often lose heart completely, and fail to put up proper resistance. It needn't even matter if the new idea isn't actually very good: the psychological effect of being caught out and dragged onto unfamiliar territory that the opponent knows well can be quite enough. World championship matches have turned on games featuring new ideas in the opening that analysis quickly showed to be harmless – but when it was too late to help the victim.

This, however, is not a book aimed at world championship candidates (though I hope they might find something of interest here too). This book is intended to help keen amateurs, club, county and tournament players to get the better of their opponents in the opening, and the ideas presented have been selected with that aim in mind.

Rules and Principles

Before we set about trying to surprise our opponents, we should consider just what surprise is and how it is caused. This subject has been discussed in detail by Amatzia Avni in his book *Surprise in Chess*, so I shall only discuss the elements relevant to the opening. Essentially, the opponent will be surprised when we don't play according to the principles that he expects us to, or that he thinks are correct. If he has been brought up on dogmatic principles, then even something like putting a knight on the edge of the board, no matter how appropriate and sensible this may be in the given situation, will probably cause some offence. Anything we can do that seems to violate *their* opening principles will tend to surprise opponents. Of course, we need to be sure that what we are doing does actually work, and is justified by the specifics of the position: if we are playing several moves with one piece, we need to be sure that the square it is aiming for is worth the cost in time. If we give up the bishop pair, then we should think our knights have good footholds from which to exert their influence, etc.

Unpromising lines and drawing lines

One of the most fertile fields for finding surprising ideas is to seek out variations for White that theory has rejected because Black can equalize, or even force a draw. Why do I say this – it seems a contradiction? The reason is that the theoretical status of such a line stems from what happened when Grandmaster X played it against Grandmaster Y. Grandmaster X decided to try a move that looked interesting and promising. Grandmaster Y thought long and hard, perhaps thought he was in trouble, and eventually, after much despair, found a defensive idea. It happens to work, and he survives to draw the game, and subsequent analysis shows that his defence was watertight, and that Grandmaster X's idea is, theoretically speaking, harmless. Other grandmasters get to know of this; the idea is not repeated and perhaps merits only a tiny footnote in the opening theory manuals – perhaps not even that, since people who write openings books are more interested in the promising lines and those where the verdict is not yet clear. Simply cataloguing "this idea leads to no advantage because of ..." is boring.

With a bit of research, especially in these modern times with databases of millions of games available, it is possible to acquaint yourself with everything (and more) that Grandmaster X knew about the line going into his game. Your opponent, unless he has happened to have studied this obscure sub-reference, will be as ignorant as Grandmaster Y was at the time. But will he defend like Grandmaster Y managed to over the board? The answer is surely no, and chances are you will come away with a handsome victory.

It is true that if you are intent on victory, then it seems unnatural to play a sequence of moves in the full knowledge that if the opponent replies in a particular way you will have to agree to a draw. From my experience though, I can testify that the ploy works well. I cannot recall a single time when the feared drawing line was actually played. On the occasions when my opponents *have* known the correct defence, they have generally deviated, either because they fear an improvement, or because they don't want to let their 'cowardly' opponent off with a draw so lightly. As Avni observed in his aforementioned book, when we fail to do what the opponent expects of us (i.e. we allow a drawish possibility when we are expected to play for a win), this surprises the opponent, affecting his judgement.

What is in this book?

Firstly, it is *not* a collection of 101 important recent theoretical novelties in topical opening lines. Interesting though such a book would be to write, it would not be of much use to many readers. Your chances of getting to play a novelty on move 26 of the Marshall Attack are fairly slim unless you are playing a specialist, who will probably already be aware of the novelty and have a reply ready, or have worked out a way to circumvent it. Besides, novelties in hot theoretical lines tend to get refuted in a few months. It is amazing how in one *Informator*, a move receives a '!!' marking. Next edition, it is only a '!?', and in some cases it receives the dreaded '?!' or worse.

Instead, I have sought out lines that the reader can expect to get a chance to play against ordinary opponents. This means at a fairly low move-number, or on a main highway of a popular opening. Many of these ideas are not going to become popular at top level, and so will not occupy a major place in opening theory books. If so, then the ideas will retain their surprise value for many years to come.

Soundness rating and surprise value

Each Surprise has two numbers (from 1 to 5) attached to it: the Soundness Rating and its Surprise Value. These indicate my estimates of how objectively correct the idea is, and to what extent it can be expected to shock your opponents. These numbers should help you to judge whether the idea is likely to be effective at your level of play. If you play at a high level, then the Soundness will be the more important. At lower levels you are unlikely to be punished for playing a slightly dubious line, and the Surprise element is more significant. However, please note that many of the ideas in this book are experimental, and it is up to the reader to judge the risks involved. Here is a key to how the numbers should be interpreted:

Soundness Rating
5   Refutation; it should win
4   Excellent; better than previous theory
3   Fairly sound and reliable
2   A bit dubious, but unrefuted
1   Health warning attached!

Surprise Value
5   An absolute shocker; a thunderbolt
4   Bewildering for all but the best prepared opponents
3   Should prove quite unnerving for a typical opponent
2   A bit surprising, but don't rely on its psychological impact
1   No real surprise value

How can I find more surprises?

Well, if this book is successful, then maybe there will be *101 More Chess Opening Surprises*... In any case, there is no reason why you shouldn't find your own opening surprises too. Seeking out forgotten lines that are considered 'theoretically harmless' is one good approach, while I can recommend finding a good source of recent games (for instance the Internet chess magazine TWIC), and quickly playing over some games. Some ideas will grab your attention, and if you analyse them carefully (ideally with other players and a computer), then you will place yourself at a considerable advantage.

This book has been a great deal of fun to write, and I hope that you will have as much fun reading it and trying out the ideas. Just choose your opponents carefully with some of them...!

Graham Burgess
January 1998, Bristol, England

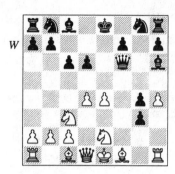

1a: after 9...fxg3

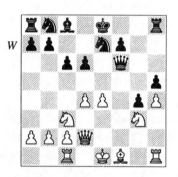

1b: after 12...♘e7

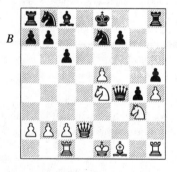

1c: after 15 dxe5

Surprise 1   **B**

Soundness: 3   Surprise Value: 3

King's Gambit: Fischer

In the Fischer Defence to the King's Gambit, after **1 e4 e5 2 f4 exf4 3 ♘f3 d6 4 d4 g5 5 h4 g4 6 ♘g1 ♝h6 7 ♘c3 c6 8 ♘ge2 ♛f6 9 g3**, Black almost invariably plays 9...f3, when 10 ♘f4 gives White good long-term attacking prospects. However, **9...fxg3!?** *(1a)* seems to have been under-rated. After **10 ♘xg3 ♝xc1 11 ♖xc1 h5!?** (instead 11...♛h6 12 ♝d3 ♛e3+ 13 ♘ce2 ♘e7 14 ♛d2 ♛xd2+ 15 ♔xd2 d5 16 ♖ce1 ♝e6 17 ♘f4 0-0 18 exd5 ♘xd5 19 ♘xe6 let White regain the pawn with an advantage in Short-Akopian, Madrid 1997) **12 ♛d2 ♘e7** *(1b)* (rather than wasting time with 12...♛h6, when White can allow the exchange of queens as he has ominous play in the centre) White has yet to establish anything convincing:

a) **13 ♝c4 ♝e6 14 e5 ♛f3 15 ♘ce4 ♝xc4 16 ♘xd6+ ♔f8 17 ♖g1 ♝e6** ∓ Avchinnikov-Susedenko, corr 1990.

b) **13 e5 dxe5 14 ♘ce4 ♛f4 15 dxe5** *(1c)* 15...♛xd2+! (the greedy and very risky 15...♛xe5 is the only move considered in the old theory books, e.g. 16 ♖d1 0-0 17 ♛g5+ ♛xg5 18 hxg5 ±) 16 ♔xd2 ♘d7 17 ♖e1 ♘g6 18 ♔c1 ♘dxe5 19 ♝g2 ♔e7 20 ♘c5 f5 21 ♘d3 ♔f6 22 ♘xe5 ♘xe5 23 ♖ef1 ♘g6 24 ♝e4 ♔xh4 25 ♖xh4 ♔g5 26 ♖hh1 f4 27 ♘e2 f3 28 ♘d4 and now **28...♝d7** seems quite good for Black. Instead **28...h4?** 29 ♘xf3+ gxf3 30 ♝xf3 ♝e6 31 ♖hg1+ ♔f6 32 ♝g4+ allowed White to escape with a draw in J.Littlewood-Desmedt, corr. 1995.

Surprise 2   W

Soundness: 2   Surprise Value: 4

King's Gambit: Rosentreter

This old gambit arises after **1 e4 e5 2 f4 exf4 3 ♘f3 g5 4 d4!?** *(2a)*.

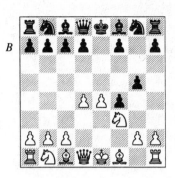

2a: after 4 d4

Now 4...h6 transposes to the Becker Defence, while 4...d6 reaches the Fischer Defence. The next Surprise will present an interesting reply to 4...g4. Here we shall focus on **4...♗g7**, when White has the entirely new idea **5 ♘c3!? d6 6 g3** *(2b)*, which you will not find in the theory books. Then:

a) **6...h6** and now, rather than **7 h4** g4 8 ♘h2 fxg3 9 ♘xg4 h5 (9...♘c6!?) 10 ♘e3 ♕f6, which looked unconvincing for White in Ramik-Oral, Czech Ch 1993, **7 gxf4** g4 8 ♘g1 ♕h4+ 9 ♔e2 g3 10 ♘f3 ♗g4 is at least OK for White.

b) **6...g4 7 ♘h4 f3** (this is similar to 4 ♗c4 ♗g7 5 0-0 h6 6 d4 d6 7 g3 g4 8 ♘h4 f3, but here White retains the possibility of castling queenside) **8 ♗e3 ♘c6 9 ♕d2** *(2c)* and now:

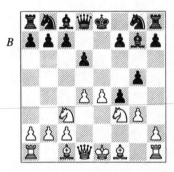

2b: after 6 g3

b1) **9...♘ge7** 10 0-0-0 0-0 11 h3 h5 12 ♗h6 gives White a strong attack.

b2) **9...♗f6** 10 ♘f5 ♗xf5 11 exf5 looks awkward for Black.

b3) **9...♘ce7** 10 0-0-0 c6 11 ♗d3 ♕a5 12 ♖he1 b5 13 ♘f5 ♗xf5 14 exf5 0-0-0 (not 14...b4 15 ♘e4 ♕xa2? 16 ♘xd6+ followed by 17 ♕xb4) 15 ♗g5 b4 16 ♘e4 ♘d5 17 ♗xd8 ♕xd8 (17...♕xa2 18 c4! bxc3 19 ♘xc3 ♘xc3 20 ♕xc3) 18 ♔b1 a5 19 ♗c4 ♘gf6 20 ♘xf6 ♗xf6 21 ♗xd5 cxd5 and now, in Furhoff-Aleksandrov, Stockholm 1995, White should have played 22 ♕d3 ♕b6 23 ♕e3 ♔d7 24 ♕h6!, which is very strong indeed.

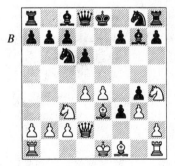

2c: after 9 ♕d2

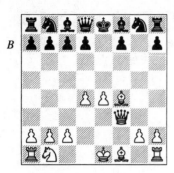

3a: after 6 ♕xf3

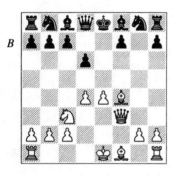

3b: after 7 ♘c3

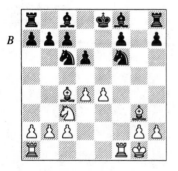

3c: after 11 0-0

Surprise 3   W

Soundness: 2   Surprise Value: 4

Rosentreter: 4...g4 5 ♗xf4

We now take a look at **1 e4 e5 2 f4 exf4 3 ♘f3 g5 4 d4!? g4**. Old theory focused on the line 5 ♘e5 ♕h4+ 6 g3 fxg3 7 ♕xg4, when 7...g2+?! 8 ♕xh4 gxh1♕ is surprisingly good for White, but the sensible 7...♕xg4 8 ♘xg4 d5 is good for Black. The new idea is **5 ♗xf4!? gxf3 6 ♕xf3** *(3a)*. This little-explored Muzio-style sacrifice is quite dangerous, with Michael Adams as one high-rated recent victim. Then:

a) **6...♗g7?!** 7 ♕g3.

b) **6...d5** is met by 7 ♘c3, going for rapid development.

c) **6...♘c6** 7 ♗c4 ♗g7 (7...d5!?) 8 e5!? ♘xd4 9 ♗xf7+! ♔xf7 10 ♕h5+ ♔f8 (Black could try 10...♔e6!?) 11 0-0, with a strong attack for White – Glazkov and Estrin.

d) **6...d6 7 ♘c3!?** *(3b)* and then:

d1) **7...♗g7** could be tried.

d2) **7...♗h6** 8 ♗c4 ♗xf4 9 ♕xf4 ♕f6 10 ♕e3 ♗e6 11 ♘d5 ♗xd5 12 ♗xd5 ♘c6 13 ♖f1 is awkward for Black, Hresc-Klavcić, Finkenstein 1992.

d3) **7...♕h4+** 8 g3 ♕g4 9 ♕e3 with good compensation after either **9...c6** 10 ♗e2 ♕h3 11 0-0-0 ♗g4 12 ♗xg4 ♕xg4 13 d5 ♘d7 14 e5 Plotnikov-Ilijin, corr 1990 or **9...♘e7** 10 ♗e2 ♕g6 11 0-0 ♗h3 12 ♖fe1 ♗g7 13 ♗d3 Rozhkov-Varianichenko, corr 1990.

d4) **7...♘c6** 8 ♗c4 ♕h4+ (8...♘xd4! 9 ♗xf7+ ♔xf7 10 ♕h5+ ♔g7 11 0-0-0 gives White fair attacking chances) 9 ♗g3 ♕f6 (9...♕e7 10 0-0) 10 ♕xf6 ♘xf6 11 0-0 *(3c)* gave Black some problems in Fedorov-Adams, Pula Echt 1997.

Surprise 4   B

Soundness: 3   Surprise Value: 3

King's Gambit: 2...♞c6, 3...f5

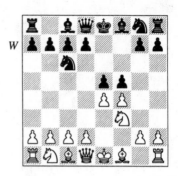

4a: after 3...f5

Here we discuss a fairly new and aggressive reply to the King's Gambit, which runs **1 e4 e5 2 f4 ♞c6 3 ♞f3 f5!?** *(4a)*. Miles and Wahls have been its main proponents (at least in written debates), while Stefan Bücker has argued White's case. First we should note that White can avoid the issue by playing 3 ♞c3, reaching a Vienna Gambit, but that is not without its problems (e.g. 3...exf4 4 ♞f3 g5 5 d4 g4 6 ♗c4 gxf3 7 0-0 ♞xd4 8 ♗xf4 ♗c5! 9 ♔h1 d6 10 ♗e3 ♗e6! *(4b)* knocked out one of White's main tries in Mi.Tseitlin-Marciano, Bucharest 1993).

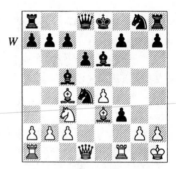

4b: after 10...♗e6

From diagram 4a White has many possible replies:

a) First of all, let's note that the e5-pawn cannot be touched just yet: **4 fxe5?** fxe4 makes White look silly, while **4 ♞xe5??** ♞xe5 5 fxe5 ♕h4+ is worse still.

b) **4 d4?!** fxe4 5 ♞xe5 is a sort of reversed Vienna where the move f2-f4 doesn't help White at all. 5...d6 6 ♞xc6 bxc6 7 ♞c3 ♞f6 gave Black good play in Schaack-Klein, 2nd Bundesliga 1993.

c) **4 d3** is unambitious. After 4...d6 5 ♗e2, Black may keep the symmetry, or break it by, e.g., 5...♗e6 6 0-0 fxe4 7 dxe4 exf4 8 ♗xf4 ♕d7 9 ♗b5 0-0-0, which gave him a reasonable game in Sundqvist-Fahad, Stockholm Rilton Cup 1996.

d) **4 ♗c4** fxe4 (4...exf4 5 d3 ♞f6 6 ♗xf4 fxe4 7 dxe4 ♕e7 8 ♞c3! Bücker) 5 ♞xe5 d5 (5...♞xe5 6 fxe5 ♕e7 is interesting) 6 ♗b5 *(4c)* and now, rather than **6...♞ge7** 7 0-0 g6 8 d3 exd3 9 ♖e1!?, which gives White the

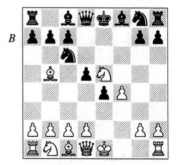

4c: after 6 ♗b5

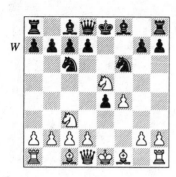

4d: after 5...♘f6

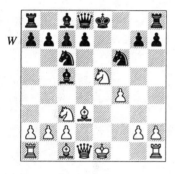

4e: after 7...♗c5

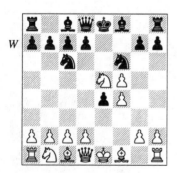

4f: after 5...♘f6

initiative (Bücker), **6...♕d6!?** looks wholly satisfactory.

e) **4 ♘c3 fxe4 5 ♘xe5 ♘f6** *(4d)* and now White must try something creative if he is not to be simply worse:

e1) **6 ♗c4 d5 7 ♘xd5!? ♘xe5 8 ♘xf6+ ♕xf6 9 fxe5 ♕xe5 10 ♕e2** is messy and unclear.

e2) **6 ♘xe4!?** can be answered with **6...♘xe5 7 ♕e2**, when White is a shade better, or the more aggressive **6...♘xe4 7 ♕h5+ g6 8 ♘xg6 hxg6.**

e3) **6 d3 exd3! 7 ♗xd3 ♗c5** *(4e)* (intending ...♕e7) 8 ♘e4 (8 ♘xc6?! bxc6 9 ♕e2+ ♔f7 and 8 ♗c4 ♕e7! 9 ♗f7+ ♔f8 both work out very well for Black) 8...♘xe5 9 ♘xc5 ♘xd3+ 10 ♕xd3 (10 ♘xd3 is drawish) 10...b6 11 ♕e3+ ♔f7 12 ♕b3+ ♔f8 13 ♘d3 ♕e7+ 14 ♔d1 d6 15 ♗d2 ♗b7 16 ♖e1 ♕f7 17 ♕xf7+ ♔xf7 18 g3 ♖ae8 gave Black a superior ending in Westerinen-Liiva, Pärnu 1996.

f) **4 exf5 e4** (the logical move, though 4...exf4 5 d4 d5 should only be a little better for White) **5 ♘e5** (5 ♘g5 ♘f6 6 d3 can be met by 6...♕e7!?, Renet-Payen, Koszalin 1997, or 6...d5 7 dxe4 dxe4) **5...♘f6** *(4f)* (5...♘xe5?! 6 fxe5 ♕e7 7 ♕h5+ ♔d8, Gallagher-Wohl, Kuala Lumpur 1992, 8 ♗c4 ♕xe5 9 ♗xg8 g6 10 ♕h3 ♖xg8 11 ♕xh7 is Bücker's analysis; Black does not have compensation) and now:

f1) **6 ♗c4 d5 7 ♗b5 ♗xf5 8 ♘xc6 bxc6 9 ♗xc6+ ♗d7** doesn't work out well for White.

f2) **6 d3** is probably best met by 6...♕e7.

f3) **6 ♘c3** and here Black should try 6...♘d4.

Surprise 5   *B*

Soundness: 1   Surprise Value: 5

King's Gambit: Capa's Barry

After **1 e4 e5 2 f4 ♗c5**, one of White's best lines is considered to be **3 ♘f3 d6 4 c3 ♗g4 5 fxe5 dxe5 6 ♕a4+**. Then 6...♘c6 is the preference of some old theory books, but after 7 ♘xe5 ♕h4+ 8 g3 ♗f2+ 9 ♔xf2 ♕f6+ 10 ♔g2 ♕xe5 11 ♗a6! Black must go into retreat, while 6...♗d7 is the normal move, and allows White a pleasant advantage after 7 ♕c2. Capablanca once played instead **6...♘d7** *(5a)*. I don't believe it to be sound, but it is interesting. I would quite understand if you chose to trust Capa's judgement rather than mine, but note the 'health warning'! After **7 ♘xe5 ♘f6** (7...♕h4+ 8 g3 ♗f2+ 9 ♔xf2 ♕f6+ is good for White) there is:

  a) **8 ♘xg4 ♘xg4 9 d4 ♕f6** (9...♕h4+ 10 g3 ♕f6 11 ♗f4; 9...0-0 – see line 'b2') 10 ♕c2 (10 dxc5 ♕f2+ 11 ♔d1 0-0-0 wins) 10...0-0-0 *(5b)* 11 ♕e2 (11 dxc5? ♘xc5 12 ♗b5 ♘xe4 13 ♖f1 ♕h4+ 14 g3 ♘xg3 wins for Black) 11...♘de5 12 ♗e3 ♘xe3 13 ♕xe3 ♘g4 14 ♕e2 (14 ♕g3 ♕g5 15 ♘d2 ♗d6 is quite good for Black) and Black doesn't seem to have enough for the pawn: 14...♕f4 (or 14...♕g5 15 ♘d2) 15 ♘d2 ♘e3 (15...♘xh2 16 0-0-0) 16 g3 ♕h6 17 ♘c4.

  b) **8 d4! 0-0** and then:

    b1) **9 ♗g5? ♘xe5 10 dxe5? ♘xe4!** *(5c)* 0-1 (11 ♗xd8 ♗f2#; 11 ♕xe4 ♕d1#) Pulvermarcher-Capablanca, New York 1907.

    b2) **9 ♘xg4 ♘xg4** and now White has a choice between the cautious 10 ♕d1 and taking the piece by 10 dxc5 ♘xc5 11 ♕d4.

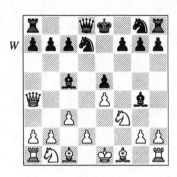

5a: after 6...♘d7

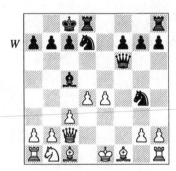

5b: after 10...0-0-0

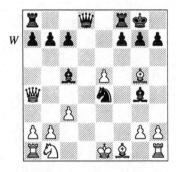

5c: after 10...♘xe4

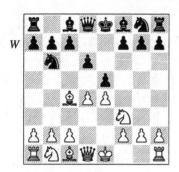

6a: after 4...♘b6

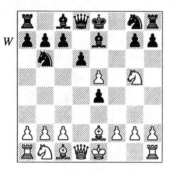

6b: after 7...♗e7

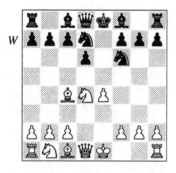

6c: after 5...♘gf6

Surprise 6   *B*

Soundness: 2   Surprise Value: 3

Philidor with an early ...♘b6

After **1 e4 e5 2 ♘f3 d6 3 d4 ♘d7, 4 ♗c4** is a very annoying move for Black. The threats against f7 restrict his options considerably – if Black wishes to maintain the pawn on e5, then he must manoeuvre carefully and passively. Here we consider two attempts by Black to play ambitiously, opening the position.

a) **4...♘b6** *(6a)* is Jeremy Sharp's idea:

a1) **5 ♗b3** exd4 6 ♕xd4 (6 ♘xd4? c5 wins a piece – the 'point'; 6 c3 dxc3 7 ♘xc3 ♗e7 doesn't give White enough for the pawn; 6 ♘g5 should be met by 6...♘h6) 6...c5 7 ♕d3 ♗e7 followed by ...♗e6 looks playable for Black.

a2) **5 ♗e2** claims that the knight is misplaced on b6. Black can then venture 5...f5!? 6 dxe5 (6 exf5 e4 7 ♘g5 ♗xf5) 6...fxe4 7 ♘g5 ♗e7 *(6b)*, when **8 ♗h5+?** g6 9 ♘xh7 is no good after 9...♗f5 or 9...♔f7, but **8 ♘xe4** dxe5 is fairly pleasant for White.

b) At Oakham 1990 Gary Quillan experimented with **4...exd4 5 ♘xd4** (5 ♕xd4 is logical, now the queen cannot be harassed by ...♘c6) **5...♘gf6** *(6c)* and now:

b1) **6 ♘c3** ♘b6 7 ♗e2 ♗e7 8 0-0 0-0 9 ♗f4 a6 10 ♖e1 c5 11 ♘f3 d5 12 exd5 ♘bxd5 13 ♘xd5 ♘xd5 14 ♗e5 ♗e6 led to a draw in his game against Kumaran.

b2) **6 0-0** ♘b6 7 ♗d3 c5 8 ♘b5 ♗e6 9 b3 (9 ♗g5 looks better) 9...a6 10 ♘5a3 d5 11 e5 and now **11...♘g4** looks OK. Instead, in Fishbein-Quillan, after **11...♘fd7** 12 f4 f5 13 c4 ♗e7 White could have won a pawn by 14 cxd5 ♘xd5 15 ♗xf5.

Surprise 7 W

Soundness: 2 Surprise Value: 3

Danish Gambit

Unsoundness is one thing that might put players off an interesting gambit, but a dull equalizing line is the one thing guaranteed to destroy a speculative line's popularity. In the Danish Gambit, **1 e4 e5 2 d4 exd4 3 c3 dxc3 4 ♗c4**, Schlechter's **4...cxb2 5 ♗xb2 d5 6 ♗xd5** *(7a)* 6...♘f6 7 ♗xf7+ ♔xf7 8 ♕xd8 ♗b4+ is fairly barren. Here are a few ideas from diagram 7a:

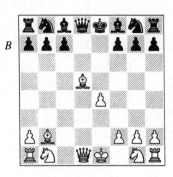

7a: after 6 ♗xd5

a) **6...♗b4+** 7 ♔f1 ♘f6 8 ♕b3 (8 ♕a4+ ♘c6 9 ♗xc6+ bxc6 10 ♕xb4?? ♕d1+ mates) 8...♕e7 9 ♘f3 ♘c6 10 a3 ♗c5 11 ♘bd2 0-0 12 ♖c1 is promising for White, Marshall-Motkovsky, Los Angeles 1903.

b) **6...♘f6 7 ♘c3!?** *(7b)* (note that this is the same as 5...♘f6 6 ♘c3 d5 7 ♗xd5):

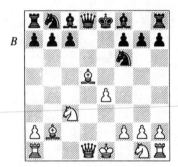

7b: after 7 ♘c3

b1) **7...♘xd5** 8 ♘xd5 (threatening 9 ♘f6+) 8...♘c6 9 ♘f3 ♗g4 10 h3 ♗h5 11 0-0 ♕d7 12 ♖b1 0-0-0 13 ♕b3 with a menacing initiative.

b2) **7...♗e7 8 ♕e2** (8 ♕f3 c6 9 ♗b3 0-0 10 ♘ge2 ♘bd7 11 ♖d1 ♕c7 12 h3 ♘c5 13 ♗c2 ♗e6 14 0-0 ♖ad8 15 ♘d4 ♘fd7 16 ♕h5 isn't enough for the pawn, Hector-Schüssler, Gothenburg 1985) **8...♘xd5 9 ♘xd5 c6 10 ♘xe7 ♕xe7 11 ♗xg7 ♖g8 12 ♗b2** *(7c)* and then:

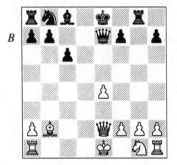

7c: after 12 ♗b2

b21) **12...♕b4+** 13 ♕d2 ♕xe4+ (or 13...♕xd2+ 14 ♔xd2 ♖xg2) 14 ♘e2 ♖xg2 15 0-0-0 is precarious for Black.

b22) **12...♖xg2** 13 ♕e3 (intending ♘e2 and 0-0-0) 13...♕g5 14 ♕xg5 ♖xg5 15 ♘f3 ♖g4 16 0-0-0 and White's initiative compensates for the sacrificed pawn, Hector-Schüssler, Malmö 1985.

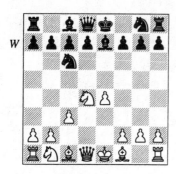

8a: after 5...♗e7

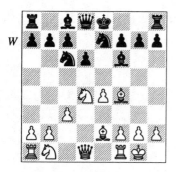

8b: after 8...♘ge7

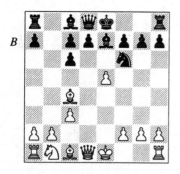

8c: after 8 e5

Surprise 8   B

Soundness: 3   Surprise Value: 3

Scotch: Malaniuk's idea

After **1 e4 e5 2 ♘f3 ♘c6 3 d4 exd4 4 ♘xd4**, Malaniuk has experimented with reasonable results with **4...♗b4+ 5 c3** (5 ♘c3 would be met by 5...♕h4) **5...♗e7** *(8a)*. Black aims to show that the pawn on c3 gets in the way of White's development and leaves light-square weaknesses:

a) **6 ♗e3 ♘f6 7 ♘d2 0-0 8 ♗e2 ♖e8!?** 9 0-0 ♗f8 10 ♗g5 h6 11 ♗h4 ♘e5 12 f4 ♘g6 puts White's centre under fire, Kiik-Malaniuk, St Petersburg 1996.

b) **6 g3 ♘f6 7 ♘xc6 bxc6 8 e5 ♘d5 9 ♗g2 ♗a6** gave Black counterplay in Yakovich-Malaniuk, Moscow Alekhine mem 1992.

c) **6 ♗e2 d6 7 ♗f4 ♗f6 8 0-0 ♘ge7** *(8b)* 9 ♘c2 0-0 10 ♘e3 ♖e8 11 ♗g3 ♘g6 and Black has no problems, Veresagin-Yandemirov, Volgograd 1994.

d) **6 ♗f4 ♗f6** looks OK for Black.

e) **6 ♗c4** and then:

e1) **6...d6** looks natural, but is actually a speculative gambit: 7 ♘xc6 bxc6 8 ♕b3 ♘f6 9 ♗xf7+ ♔f8 10 e5 (10 ♗e6 ♘xe4 is quite OK for Black) 10...♘d7 and now 11 exd6!? is critical.

e2) **6...♘f6 7 ♘xc6 bxc6 8 e5** *(8c)* 8...♘d5 (8...♘e4 9 ♕f3 d5 10 exd6 ♘xd6 11 0-0 0-0 looks reasonable too, Menacher-Zude, German Ch (Gladenbach) 1997) has been played in several games. If White grabs a pawn on d5, Black has excellent compensation: 9 ♗xd5 (9 ♕g4!? ♔f8 10 ♕f3 ♖b8!?) 9...cxd5 10 ♕xd5 ♗a6 11 c4 c6 12 ♕e4 0-0 13 0-0 f6 Kholmov-Malaniuk, Katowice 1993.

Surprise 9   *B*

Soundness: 3   Surprise Value: 3

Scotch 4 Knights: 5...♘xe4

After **1 e4 e5 2 ♘c3 ♘f6 3 ♘f3 ♘c6 4 d4 exd4 5 ♘xd4**, although far from new, the move **5...♘xe4** *(9a)* will take many players by surprise. After **6 ♘xe4** (6 ♘xc6 ♘xc3 7 ♘xd8 ♘xd1 8 ♘xf7 ♔xf7 is safe for Black) **6...♕e7** there is:

   a) **7 ♗e2 ♕xe4 8 ♘b5 ♗b4+ 9 c3 ♗a5** holds everything together for Black.

   b) **7 ♕d3 d5 8 ♘xc6 bxc6 9 ♗g5 f6 10 0-0-0 fxg5 11 ♘g3 ♔f7 12 ♗e2 g6** is good for Black, Baum-Kotan, Bad Ragaz 1993.

   c) **7 ♘b5 ♕xe4+ 8 ♗e2 ♗b4+ 9 c3 ♗a5 10 0-0 0-0 11 ♗e3 a6** *(9b)* **12 a4!?** (12 ♘d4 gives White some compensation – Turner) **12...axb5 13 axb5 ♘e5 14 ♖a4 ♕g6** and now **15 f4 ♖e8** could be tried, while **15 b4 d6 16 ♗h5** (16 bxa5 ♗f5) **16...♕f5 17 bxa5 ♘d3** is quite unclear. Instead **15 ♗h5?! ♕e6 16 ♗d4 d6** (16...♘c4!) **17 f4 ♗d7 18 ♗e2 c5 19 ♗xe5** (19 ♗f2 ♘g4) **19...dxe5 20 f5 ♕h6 21 ♗c4 ♖fd8 22 ♕d5 ♗e6** led to a win for Black in Hebden-Turner, Cambridge 1995.

   d) **7 f3 d5** *(9c)* and then:

   d1) **8 ♘xc6 bxc6** and here **9 ♕e2 dxe4 10 ♕xe4 ♕xe4+ 11 fxe4 ♗d6 12 c4 ♔e7** is equal (*ECO*), while after **9 ♗d3 dxe4**, White should try **10 fxe4**, as **10 ♗xe4? f5 11 ♗g5 ♕e5!** 12 ♕d8+ ♔f7 should win for Black, A.Gatine-Goehl, Duisburg girls U-18 Wch 1992.

   d2) **8 ♗b5 ♗d7 9 0-0 dxe4 10 ♗xc6 bxc6 11 ♖e1 0-0-0 12 ♖xe4 ♕f6 13 ♕e2 ♗c5** (13...c5 14 ♘b3 ♗c6 15 ♕a6+ is also possible) **14 ♗e3 ♖he8** looks OK for Black.

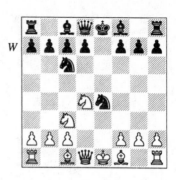

9a: after 5...♘xe4

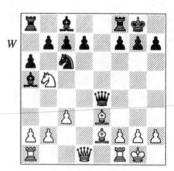

9b: after 11...a6

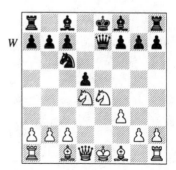

9c: after 7...d5

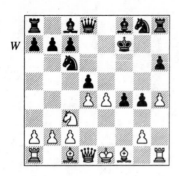

10a: after 8...d5

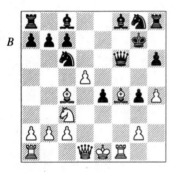

10b: after 12 ♖f1

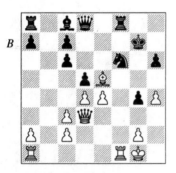

10c: after 15 ♕d3

Surprise 10   W

Soundness: 3 Surprise Value: 2

Hamppe-Allgaier Gambit

This rather scary-sounding name refers to the following rather scary line of the Vienna Gambit: **1 e4 e5 2 ♘c3 ♘c6 3 f4 exf4 4 ♘f3 g5 5 h4 g4 6 ♘g5 h6 7 ♘xf7 ♔xf7 8 d4**. The main line is then **8...d5** *(10a)*, offering a pawn to gain some time, as introduced by the young Capablanca in his match against Corzo. White should continue **9 ♗xf4**:

a) **9...dxe4** 10 ♗c4+ ♔g7 11 d5 ♕f6 12 ♖f1 *(10b)* 12...♘e5 (12...♗b4 13 dxc6 ♗xc3+ 14 bxc3 ♕xc3+ 15 ♕d2 ♕xa1+ 16 ♔e2 and 12...♘a5 13 ♘xe4 are good for White) 13 ♘xe4 ♕xh4+ 14 ♗g3 ♕h5 15 d6 cxd6 (15...♗xd6 16 ♕d4 wins for White) 16 ♕d5 ♘f3+ 17 gxf3 ♕xd5 18 ♗xd5 offers White an edge.

b) **9...♗b4** is the theoretical main line:

b1) **10 ♗e2?!** ♗xc3+ 11 bxc3 ♘f6 12 0-0 ♔g7 13 c4 ♘xe4 14 cxd5 ♕xh4 15 dxc6 ♖e8! ∓ Konikowski.

b2) **10 ♗d3?!** ♘f6 11 0-0 ♗xc3 12 bxc3 ♔g7 13 exd5 ♕xd5 14 ♕d2 ♕h5 15 ♕f2 ♖f8 16 ♖ab1 a6 17 ♗xc7 leaves Black a little tied up, but I doubt it is worth the material.

b3) **10 ♗b5** ♗xc3+ 11 bxc3 ♘f6 12 0-0 ♔g7 13 ♗xc6 bxc6 14 ♗e5 ♖f8 15 ♕d3 *(10c)* 15...a5 (the ...♗a6 resource is vital to stop White's rooks *both* invading on the f-file) 16 exd5 cxd5 (16...♗a6 17 c4 cxd5 18 h5 wins for White) 17 ♖ae1 ♗a6 18 ♕f5 and now **18...♗xf1** 19 ♕xg4+ ♔h8 20 ♖xf1! ♗a6 21 ♕g6 ♕e7 22 ♕xh6+ ♔g8 23 g4! is promising for White, but **18...♗c8!** gives White nothing better than 19 ♕d3, when 19...♗a6 repeats.

Surprise 11 *W*

Soundness: 2   Surprise Value: 4

Hamppe-Allgaier: 8 ♗c4+

After **1 e4 e5 2 ♘c3 ♘c6 3 f4 exf4 4 ♘f3 g5 5 h4 g4 6 ♘g5 h6 7 ♘xf7 ♔xf7**, White has another interesting possibility: **8 ♗c4+** *(11a)*. After **8...d5**, Shulman has shown that **9 ♗xd5+** is a dangerous try. (Instead 9 ♘xd5!? ♔g7 is considered suspect for White, but 10 d4 ♘f6 11 ♗xf4 ♗d6 12 ♘xf6 ♕xf6 13 ♗e3 ♗g3+ 14 ♔e2 ♖d8 15 c3 ♗xh4 16 ♖f1 ♕g6 17 ♖f7+ ♔h8 18 ♕h1! ♗g5 19 ♗xg5 ♕xg5 20 ♖af1 ♗d7 21 ♖1f6 h5 *(11b)* 22 ♕h4!! ♕xh4 23 ♖h6+ ♔g8 24 ♖xd7+ ♔f8 25 ♖h8# (1-0) Black-burne-Benfy, Manchester 1898 is worth noting.) Then Shulman-Marciano, Ubeda 1997 proceeded **9...♔g7 10 d4** (10 b4, to free b2 for the bishop, is a crazed attacking alternative) **10...♘f6** (10...f3 11 gxf3 is messy, and probably the critical line) **11 ♗xf4 ♗b4 12 ♗xc6 bxc6 13 0-0 ♖f8** (13...♗a6? 14 ♗e5 wins) **14 ♕d2 ♘g8** (14...♘xe4 15 ♗xh6+ ♔h7 16 ♕e3 gives White nice attacking prospects) **15 ♗e5+ ♔h7 16 ♖xf8 ♕xf8** (16...♗xf8 17 ♖f1 ♕e8 18 ♕f4 ♗a6 19 ♕f7+ ♕xf7 20 ♖xf7+ ♔g6 21 ♖xc7 ♘e7 22 ♗d6 gives White too many pawns for the piece) **17 ♖f1 ♕e7 18 ♕f4 ♗e6** *(11c)* (18...♗xc3?! 19 bxc3 ♗e6 20 d5) **19 ♘d5!!** (the idea is to free a square for the queen on the b1-h7 diagonal) **19...♗d2 20 ♕xd2 cxd5 21 ♕f4!? c6 22 exd5 cxd5 23 c4 ♕d7** (23...♕b7 24 ♕f2 ♘e7 25 ♕f6 is a neat win) **24 h5 ♘e7** (24...♖c8 25 b3! makes sure the queen will have a check on c2 after 26 ♕f2) **25 ♕f6 ♖g8 26 ♕f7+ 1-0.**

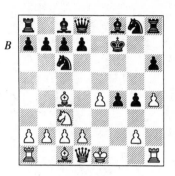

11a: after 8 ♗c4+

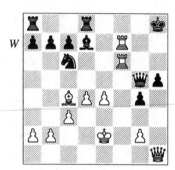

11b: after 21...h5

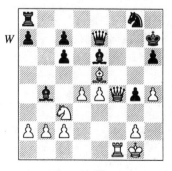

11c: after 18...♗e6

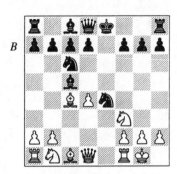

12a: after 7 cxd4

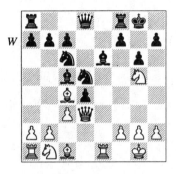

12b: after 10...g6

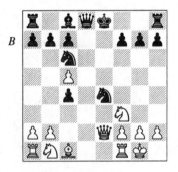

12c: after 9 ♕e2

Surprise 12   W

Soundness: 3   Surprise Value: 3

Italian Game: 5 d4 and 6 0-0

Our theme position here is **1 e4 e5 2 ♘f3 ♘c6 3 ♗c4 ♗c5 4 c3 ♘f6 5 d4 exd4 6 0-0 ♘xe4** (see below for other moves) **7 cxd4** *(12a)*, which can be reached via several other move-orders, viz. 1 e4 e5 2 ♘f3 ♘c6 3 ♗c4 ♗c5 4 c3 ♘f6 5 0-0 ♘xe4 6 d4 exd4 7 cxd4, 1 e4 e5 2 ♘f3 ♘c6 3 d4 exd4 4 ♗c4 ♗c5 5 0-0 ♘f6 6 c3 ♘xe4 7 cxd4, 1 e4 e5 2 ♘f3 ♘c6 3 ♗c4 ♘f6 4 d4 exd4 5 0-0 ♗c5 6 c3 ♘xe4 7 cxd4. Deviations for Black from our main move-order on move 6 cannot be recommended:

a) **6...dxc3?** 7 e5 ±.

b) **6...d5?!** 7 exd5 ♘xd5 8 ♖e1+ ♗e6 9 ♘g5 0-0 10 ♕d3 g6 *(12b)* 11 ♖xe6 fxe6 12 ♕h3 ♕e7 13 ♕xe6+ ♕xe6 14 ♘xe6 +− Estrin-Letić, corr. 1967-9.

c) **6...d3?!** 7 b4!? ♗e7 8 e5 ♘g4 9 ♖e1 d6 10 exd6 ±.

From diagram 12a:

a) **7...♗e7?!** 8 d5 ♘b8 9 ♖e1 ♘d6 (9...♘f6? 10 d6 cxd6 11 ♗g5 0-0 12 ♖xe7! ♕xe7 13 ♘c3 +−) 10 ♗d3 0-0 11 ♘c3 ±.

b) **7...d5!** 8 dxc5 dxc4 9 ♕e2 *(12c)* (9 ♕xd8+ ♔xd8 is harmless) and now:

b1) **9...♕e7** 10 ♕xc4 ♘xc5 11 b4 ♘e6 12 b5 (rather than 12 ♗a3 a6 13 ♘c3 ♗d7 14 ♘d5 ♕d8 15 ♖ad1 0-0 16 ♖fe1 b5 V.Ivanov-P.Jorgensen, corr. 1986-91) 12...♘a5 (12...♕b4 13 ♕e2 ♘e7 14 ♗a3 ♕a5 15 ♘e5 left Black tied up in a 1996 game between two strong computers) 13 ♕c3 ± ♕f6? 14 ♕xa5 ♕xa1 15 ♘c3 +−.

b2) **9...♕d3** is seen in the next Surprise.

Surprise 13 W

Soundness: 3   Surprise Value: 3

Italian Game: 9...♕d3

After **1 e4 e5 2 ♘f3 ♘c6 3 ♗c4 ♗c5 4 c3 ♘f6 5 d4 exd4 6 0-0 ♘xe4 7 cxd4 d5! 8 dxc5 dxc4 9 ♕e2**, for a long time, **9...♕d3!?** was considered a complete answer. However, things are not so clear after **10 ♖e1** *(13a)*:

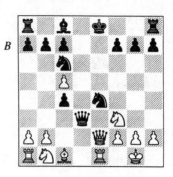

13a: after 10 ♖e1

a) **10...♕xe2 11 ♖xe2** is good for White: **11...♗f5? 12 g4!** *(13b)*, winning a piece, has occurred in a number of games; **11...f5 12 ♘bd2 0-0 13 ♘xe4 fxe4 14 ♖xe4 ±**.

b) **10...f5 11 ♘c3 0-0 12 ♘xe4 fxe4 13 ♕xe4 ♗f5 14 ♕h4!?** *(13c)* and then:

b1) **14...♕d5 15 ♗e3** (15 ♗d2 intending ♗c3 and kingside play looks tempting) **15...♖ad8 16 ♖ac1 ♗d3**. Now Black is threatening the exchange sacrifice 17...♖xf3, so **17 ♕g3** is in order.

b2) **14...♖ad8 15 ♗e3** (15 ♗g5!? is also possible) **15...♕d5** is line 'b1'.

b3) **14...♖ae8 15 ♗f4 ♕d5** (15...♕d7 is equal according to Schüssler, but it's hard to believe White doesn't have something after 16 ♖ad1) **16 ♗xc7 ♕xc5 17 ♕g3 ♕d5 18 ♗d6 ♖xe1+ 19 ♖xe1 ♖d8 20 ♗e7 ♖e8 21 ♗f6 ♖xe1+ 22 ♘xe1** (queens and opposite-coloured bishops favour the player with the safer king, i.e. White here, but it's no more than a nagging edge) **22...♕d7 23 ♗c3 b5 24 a3 a5 25 h3 ♗e4?!** (25...b4? drops a pawn to 26 axb4 axb4 27 ♗xb4 ♘xb4 28 ♕b8+, but 25...h6 should be OK) **26 ♕f4 ♕e7 27 ♕e3 a4? 28 ♘f3 ♗xf3 29 ♕xf3 ♕d7 30 ♕e4 ♘e7 31 ♕e5** gave White a more serious edge in Biolek-Keitlinghaus, Ostrava 1993.

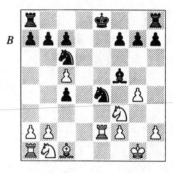

13b: after 12 g4

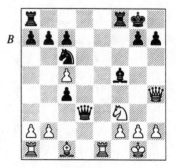

13c: after 14 ♕h4

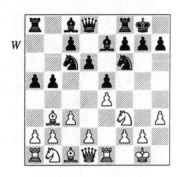

14a: after 9...a5

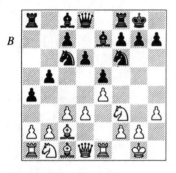

14b: after 11 ♗c2

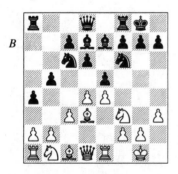

14c: after 12 ♗d3

Surprise 14   B

Soundness: 3   Surprise Value: 2

Closed Spanish: 9...a5

After **1 e4 e5 2 ♘f3 ♘c6 3 ♗b5 a6 4 ♗a4 ♘f6 5 0-0 ♗e7 6 ♖e1 b5 7 ♗b3 0-0 8 c3 d6 9 h3**, the rare **9...a5** *(14a)* is much less well analysed than the other plausible moves here. It is far from bad, though full equality is hard to achieve. Here are some interesting lines:

a) **10 a4** b4 11 ♗c4 ♗b7 12 d3 h6 13 ♘bd2 d5! 14 exd5 ♘xd5 15 ♘xe5 ♘xe5 16 ♖xe5 ♗f6 ∓ Campanella-Lane, Brussels 1995.

b) **10 a3** a4 11 ♗c2 ♗d7 12 d4 ♖e8 13 ♘bd2 ♗f8 14 ♘d3 ♘a5 15 ♖b1 c5 16 d5 c4 17 ♗c2 ♘b3 conquered a great deal of queenside territory in Kwiatkowski-Lane, London 1994.

c) **10 d3 a4 11 ♗c2** *(14b)* and now:

c1) **11...♗d7** 12 ♘bd2 ♖e8 13 ♘f1 ♗f8 (Kruppa-I.Zaitsev, Minsk 1993) 14 d4 ±.

c2) **11...♗e6** 12 ♘bd2 d5 13 exd5 ♕xd5 14 ♕e2 ♖fe8 = Borsany-Bernstein, corr 1963.

d) **10 d4 a4 11 ♗c2 ♗d7** (11...♖e8!? 12 ♘a3 ♖b8 13 c4?! ♘xd4 14 ♘xd4 exd4 15 cxb5 d5 is messy, S.Garcia-Wade, Havana Capablanca mem 1964) and:

d1) **12 ♗e3** exd4 13 cxd4 ♘b4 is quite all right for Black.

d2) **12 ♘bd2!?** ♖e8 13 ♘f1 ♗f8 14 ♘g3 h6 15 ♘h2 ♘a5 16 f4 ♘c4 17 ♖b1 c5 is fine for Black, Wolff-Razuvaev, New York 1989.

d3) **12 ♗d3!?** *(14c)* 12...♕b8 (perhaps 12...exd4!?) 13 ♘a3 exd4 14 cxd4 ♘b4 15 ♗b1 ♕b7 16 ♗g5 ♖ad8 17 ♘c2 ♘c6 18 ♘e3 ♖fe8 ± Renet-Agdestein, Lyons 1988.

Surprise 15   *B*

Soundness: 3   Surprise Value: 3

Berlin with 4...♗e7 and ...d6

The Berlin Defence to the Spanish, **1 e4 e5 2 ♘f3 ♘c6 3 ♗b5 ♘f6** deserves to be a bit more popular. A big practical plus-point is that White is denied the possibility of playing the Exchange Variation (3...a6 4 ♗xc6).

The cautious **4 d3** can be answered by Motwani's idea **4...♘e7!?** *(15a)*, intending ...♘g6, ...c6, and ...d5. 5 ♘xe5? due to 5...c6, winning a piece after 6 ♗c4 ♕a5+ or 6 ♘c4 ♘g6 7 ♗a4 b5. Note that this idea doesn't work in the analogous line 3...a6 4 ♗a4 ♘f6 5 d3.

The main line is **4 0-0**, when I propose Black investigate **4...♗e7** *(15b)*. This move looks passive and insignificant, which just adds to the surprise value when Black follows it up aggressively. Now **5 ♘c3 d6 6 ♗xc6+ bxc6 7 d4 exd4** doesn't give White much after either **8 ♕xd4** 0-0 9 ♖e1 ♗g4 10 ♕d3 ♗xf3 11 ♕xf3 ♘d7 12 b3 ♗f6 or **8 ♘xd4** ♗d7 9 ♕f3 0-0 10 h3 ♖b8 11 b3 ♖e8 12 ♗b2 ♗f8 13 ♖fe1 c5 14 ♘f5 g6 15 ♘e3 ♗g7 = Short-Portisch, Skellefteå 1989, so the normal move is **5 ♖e1**, when I suggest **5...d6** *(15c)*, which Short has played with success:

a) **6 d4 exd4 7 ♘xd4 ♗d7** and now:

a1) **8 ♗xc6** bxc6 9 c4 0-0 10 ♘c3 ♖e8 11 b3 h6 12 ♗f4 c5 13 ♘f3 ♗c6 14 h3 ♘d7 intending ...♗f6 was OK for Black in Ivanchuk-Short, Linares 1995.

a2) **8 ♘c3** 0-0 9 ♘f3 ♘e5 10 ♗xd7 ♘xf3+ 11 ♕xf3 ♘xd7 12 ♘d5 ♘b6 with equality, Luther-Portisch, Groningen FIDE Wch 1997.

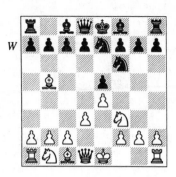

15a: after 4...♘e7

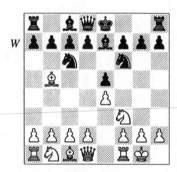

15b: after 4...♗e7

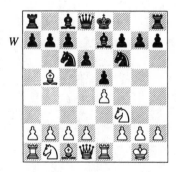

15c: after 5...d6

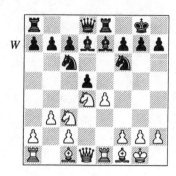

15d: after 10...d5

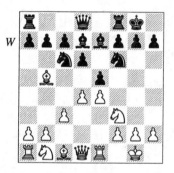

15e: after 7...♗d7

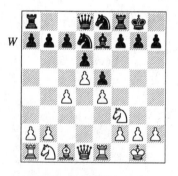

15f: after 10...♘e8

a3) **8 ♗f1** 0-0 9 ♘c3 ♖e8 (9...♘xd4 10 ♕xd4 ♗c6 11 ♗f4 ♘d7 could be tried) 10 b3 d5! *(15d)* 11 exd5 (Ivanchuk-Short, Novgorod 1994) and now Black should have played 11...♘b4 12 ♗c4 ♗c5, when 13 ♘e6 is White's only try.

b) **6 c3 0-0** and then:

b1) **7 d3** a6 8 ♗a4 ♘d7 9 d4 ♗f6 10 ♗c2 ♘b6 11 h3 ♗d7 12 b3!? (12 ♘a3 ♘e7 13 ♗e3 ♘g6 14 ♕d2 ♕e7 15 ♖ad1 ♖ad8 16 ♕c1 h6 gave Black satisfactory play in Nunn-Morozevich, Amsterdam Donner mem 1995) 12...exd4 13 cxd4 ♘b4 14 ♘c3 ♘xc2 15 ♕xc2 c6 16 ♗a3 ♗e7 17 ♖ad1 ♖e8 18 d5 cxd5 19 exd5 ♖c8 20 ♕d3 h6 21 ♘e4 ♗f5 22 ♕d4 ♗f8 23 ♘g3 ♖xe1+ 24 ♖xe1 ♗h7 25 ♘h5 (Shirov-Short, Dos Hermanas 1997) 25...♖c2!? is OK for Black.

b2) **7 d4 ♗d7** *(15e)* sets a little trap, into which some strong players have fallen, as 8...♘xd4 is threatened.

b21) **8 ♘bd2?!** duly allows 8...♘xd4 9 cxd4 ♗xb5.

b22) **8 ♕e2** ♖e8 9 d5 ♘b8 10 ♗xd7 ♘bxd7 11 c4 is similar to Illescas-Short below, but the white queen is exposed to possible attack on e2, while the black rook is getting in the way on e8, J.Polgar-Short, Moscow OL 1994.

b23) **8 d5** ♘b8 9 ♗xd7 (it seems logical to exchange the 'bad' bishop, but Black now coordinates his forces well) 9...♘bxd7 10 c4 ♘e8!? *(15f)* (Short goes directly for kingside play) 11 ♘c3 g6 12 ♖b1?! (12 ♗h6 ♘g7 13 ♕d2 a5!? planning ...♘c5) 12...f5 13 b4?! (13 exf5 gxf5 14 ♗h6 ♖f6! 15 ♗g5 ♖g6 16 ♗xe7 ♕xe7 gives counterplay) 13...f4! 14 a4 ♖f7 15 ♗a3 g5 16 ♘d2 ♘ef6 17 f3 ♖g7 18 ♔h1 g4 19 ♕e2 ♕h8 20 ♖ec1 ♖g6! gave Black a powerful kingside attack in Illescas-Short, Dos Hermanas 1997.

Surprise 16   *B*

Soundness: 1   Surprise Value: 5

Spanish: Bulgarian Defence

Here we have one of the most horrifying ideas in the book: **1 e4 e5 2 ♘f3 ♘c6 3 ♗b5 a5** *(16a)*. However, the low soundness rating is due only to a feeling that it can't really be good – no one has demonstrated any clear refutation, tactical or otherwise.

a) **4 a3** (attempting to ignore Black's play...) 4...♘f6 5 0-0 ♗c5 6 c3 0-0 7 d4 ♗a7 (...but Black finds a way to put ...a5 to use) 8 ♗g5 h6 9 ♗h4 d6 10 ♕d3 ♕e7 11 ♘bd2 ♘d8 and Black went on to take the initiative in Vekan-G.Popov, corr. 1991.

b) **4 0-0 ♘a7** *(16b)* is 'the point':

b1) **5 ♗a4?!** b5 6 ♗b3 a4 traps the bishop (7 ♗xf7+ is inadequate).

b2) **5 ♗c4** b5 6 ♗e2 d6 7 d4 ♗g4 8 a4 b4 9 c3 ♗e7 10 ♘bd2 bxc3 11 bxc3 exd4 12 cxd4 ♘f6 13 h3 ♗d7 14 ♗c4 0-0 with an interesting, unbalanced position in Simons-G.Welling, Eindhoven 1993.

b3) **5 ♗e2 d6 6 d4 ♗g4** *(16c)* and then:

b31) **7 ♘c3** should be met by **7...♗e7** 8 dxe5 ♗xf3 or **7...♗xf3** 8 ♗xf3 ♘f6.

b32) **7 dxe5 ♗xf3** 8 ♗xf3 dxe5 9 ♕d2 (the exchange of queens does not displace the black king, as is so often the case in such lines) 9...♘f6 10 c3 ♗c5 11 ♕b3 b6 12 ♖d1 0-0 13 ♘c4 ♕e8 with no problems for Black, J.Kuczynski-G.Popov, corr. 1991.

c) **4 ♘c3** may be best met by 4...♗b4, intending ...♘ge7. This is similar to the Alapin, 3...♗b4?!, except that the bishop now actually hits a knight, and is defended.

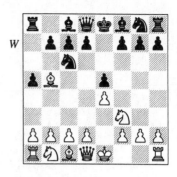

16a: after 3...a5

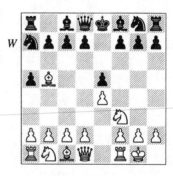

16b: after 4...♘a7

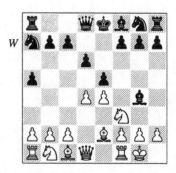

16c: after 6...♗g4

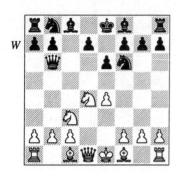

17a: after 5...♕b6

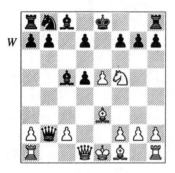

17b: after 9...♕xb2

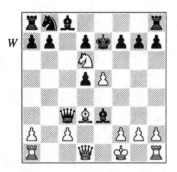

17c: after 12...♔e7

Surprise 17   B

Soundness: 3   Surprise Value: 4

Sicilian: Gaw-Paw

This oddly-named variation of the Sicilian is a Swedish invention. It arises after the moves **1 e4 c5 2 ♘f3 e6 3 d4 cxd4 4 ♘xd4 ♘f6 5 ♘c3 ♕b6** *(17a)*. The critical line runs **6 e5** (for 6 ♘b3, see the next Surprise) **6...♗c5 7 ♗e3 ♘d5 8 ♘xd5 exd5 9 ♘f5 ♕xb2!** *(17b)*:

a) **10 ♘d6+ ♗xd6 11 exd6 ♕b4+** gives Black one solid extra pawn (once White has regained the d5-pawn).

b) **10 ♘xg7+ ♔d8** is no great problem, as Black's king has the c7-square.

c) **10 f4 ♗xe3 11 ♘xe3 ♕b4+ 12 ♕d2 ♕xf4 13 ♘xd5 ♕xe5+ 14 ♕e2 ♕xe2+ 15 ♗xe2 ♔d8 16 0-0 d6** and White's compensation is wholly inadequate.

d) **10 ♗xc5 ♕c3+ 11 ♔e2** (11 ♕d2 ♕xa1+ 12 ♔e2 ♕xe5+ is no good for White) **11...♕xc5 12 ♘d6+ ♔f8 13 f4** (13 ♕d2 ♘c6 14 ♕f4 ♕xc2+ 15 ♔e3 ♕c3+ 16 ♗d3 ♘xe5; 13 ♘xc8 ♘c6! 14 ♘d6 ♘xe5 15 ♘f5 ♖e8 with a winning attack) **13...♘c6 14 ♔f3 f6! 15 ♘xc8 fxe5 16 fxe5 ♘xe5+ 17 ♔f4 ♖xc8 18 ♔xe5 ♖e8+ 19 ♔f5 ♖e4 20 ♕f3 ♕e7 0-1** Skripchenko-P.Cramling, Belgrade wom 1996.

e) **10 ♗d3 ♕c3+ 11 ♔f1 ♗xe3 12 ♘d6+** (J.Diaz-Bellon, Cienfuegos Capablanca mem 1996) **12...♔e7!** *(17c)* (12...♔d8? 13 ♘xf7+ ♔c7 14 ♘xh8 is given as +– in *ECO*, as if it were a forced line after 6 e5) **13 ♘f5+ ♔d8 14 ♘xe3 ♕xe5** gives White some compensation for the pawns, but Black's position is fairly solid, while White's king is poorly placed too.

Surprise 18   *B*

Soundness: 3   Surprise Value: 3

Gaw-Paw (2)

1 e4 c5 2 ♘f3 e6 3 d4 cxd4 4 ♘xd4 ♘f6 5 ♘c3 ♕b6 6 ♘b3 offers Black a transposition, via 6...♘c6, to a position normally reached via the move-order 2...♘c6 3 d4 cxd4 4 ♘xd4 ♕b6 5 ♘b3 ♘f6 6 ♘c3, but with our move-order Black has avoided some annoying alternatives that White has along the way. Here we shall investigate the alternative **6...♗b4** *(18a)*.

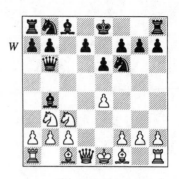

18a: after 6...♗b4

Then after **7 ♗d3** Black can try:

a) **7...♗xc3+ 8 bxc3 d6 9 0-0 ♘bd7 10 ♔h1 ♕c7 11 ♗a3 0-0 12 f4** *(18b)* seemed to give White attacking chances in Istratescu-Badea, Bucharest 1996 but now Badea analysed:

a1) **12...e5!?** 13 fxe5! (13 ♕d2 ♖e8 with the point that after 14 fxe5 dxe5 White's minor pieces are poorly placed) 13...♘xe5 14 ♘d4 ♗d7 and then **15 ♕e1 ♖fe8** (intending ...d5) 16 ♕g3? ♕xc3, or **15 ♕d2 ♖fe8 16 ♖ae1**.

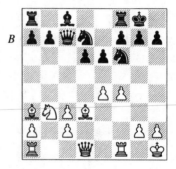

18b: after 12 f4

a2) **12...♖e8!?** (intending ...b6 followed by ...♗b7), when White should go in for 13 ♘d4 a6 14 ♕d2 b6, though Black's game is not at all bad, since 13 e5?! dxe5 14 ♗d6 ♕xc3 15 ♖f3 e4 16 ♗xe4 can be met by 16...♕c4, while 16...♘xe4 17 ♖xc3 ♘f2+ 18 ♔g1 ♘xd1 is good too.

b) **7...d5 8 exd5 ♘xd5 9 0-0 ♘xc3 10 bxc3 ♗xc3 11 ♖b1** (Fogarasi-Varga, Budapest 1995) 11...♕c7 12 ♗a3 *(18c)* is quite dangerous, but by no means hopeless for Black.

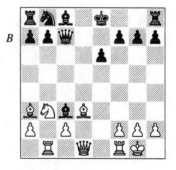

18c: after 12 ♗a3

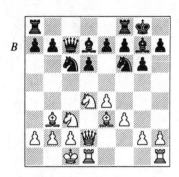

19a: after 11 ♗b3

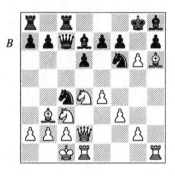

19b: after 15 hxg6

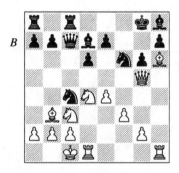

19c: after 16 ♕g5

Surprise 19   W

Soundness: 4   Surprise Value: 2

Yugoslav Attack: 10...♕c7

Our position of interest here arises after **1 e4 c5 2 ♘f3 d6 3 d4 cxd4 4 ♘xd4 ♘f6 5 ♘c3 g6 6 ♗e3 ♗g7 7 f3 0-0 8 ♕d2 ♘c6 9 ♗c4 ♗d7 10 0-0-0 ♕c7** (instead of 10...♕a5). I believe the following analysis casts grave doubt on the viability of **10...♕c7**. Essentially, Black needs to be able to avoid the exchange of dark-squared bishops and to get in ...♘c4 for this line to work, but there are tactical problems.

White plays **11 ♗b3** *(19a)* **11...♖fc8** (11...♘a5 12 ♗h6 ♘c4 and the equivalent 11...♘e5 12 ♗h6 ♘c4 are discussed in the next Surprise) **12 h4! ♘e5 13 ♗h6** (13 h5 ♘c4 is less critical) **13...♗h8** (for what happens if Black does not move his bishop, compare the next Surprise) **14 h5 ♘c4 15 hxg6!** *(19b)* is not just a move played to be flashy – White cannot be forced to take the c4-knight at all, and this frustrates both Black's counterattacking and defensive ideas:

a) **15...♘xd2??** 16 gxf7#.

b) **15...hxg6?** 16 ♗xc4 ♕xc4 17 ♗f8! ♖xf8 18 ♖xh8+! ♔xh8 19 ♕h6+ ♔g8 20 ♘d5.

c) **15...fxg6** (forced) and now, rather than the cooperative line 16 ♗xc4+ ♕xc4 17 ♗g5 ♕f7 (the queen can defend and counterattack) given in some old books, **16 ♕g5!** *(19c)* gives White a strong attacking position. Ideas include ♘f5, ♘d5 and threats to the pinned knight on c4. 16 ♗g5! is also possible.

Surprise 20   W

Soundness: 4   Surprise Value: 2

Yugoslav: 10...♕c7 (2)

The key position comes about after **1 e4 c5 2 ♘f3 d6 3 d4 cxd4 4 ♘xd4 ♘f6 5 ♘c3 g6 6 ♗e3 ♗g7 7 f3 0-0 8 ♕d2 ♘c6 9 ♗c4 ♗d7 10 0-0-0 ♕c7 11 ♗b3 ♘e5** (11...♘a5 12 ♗h6 ♘c4 is the same) **12 ♗h6!?** ♘c4 (here White must exchange, but Black has lost the option of ...♗h8) **13 ♗xc4 ♕xc4 14 h4 b5 15 ♗xg7 ♔xg7** *(20a)* and now there are two ideas:

a) **16 ♔b1** (probably best) can, it has been claimed, be answered by 16...e6 17 h5 b4 18 hxg6 fxg6. However, after 19 ♘cb5! ♗xb5 20 b3 *(20b)* White regains the piece with heavy pressure against Black's weak pawns.

b) **16 h5 b4 17 ♘d5 ♘xd5** (17...♕xa2 18 ♘b3 ♘xd5 19 hxg6 ♘f6 20 e5 dxe5 21 ♕h6+ ♔g8 22 ♖xd7 fxg6 23 ♖xe7 ♖f7 24 ♖e6) **18 hxg6!** ♘f6 (18...fxg6 19 ♕h6+) **19 ♕h6+ ♔g8 20 g7 ♖fc8 21 g4** *(20c)* provides a test of Black's defensive abilities:

b1) **21...♕xa2?** 22 g5 ♕a1+ 23 ♔d2 ♕xb2 24 ♔e1 +−.

b2) **21...e5 22 g5 exd4 23 ♔b1** and now:

b21) **23...d3?** 24 cxd3 ♕c2+ 25 ♔a1.

b22) **23...♗e6?** 24 gxf6 ♕xa2+ 25 ♔c1 ♖xc2+ 26 ♔xc2 ♖c8+ (26...♕b3+ 27 ♔d2 ♕xb2+ 28 ♔e1 ♕c3+ 29 ♔f2) 27 ♔d3 ♕b3+ 28 ♔e2.

b23) **23...♕xc2+!** 24 ♔a1 ♘h5! (24...♕g2 25 ♕xf6; 24...♗f5 25 gxf6) 25 ♕xh5 ♗f5! 26 exf5 ♕xf5 should survive.

20a: after 15...♔xg7

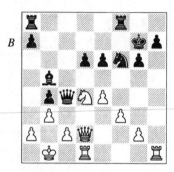

20b: after 20 b3

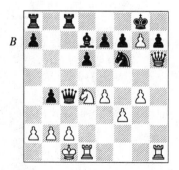

20c: after 21 g4

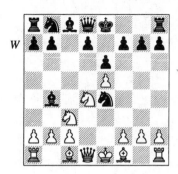

21a: after 6...♘e4

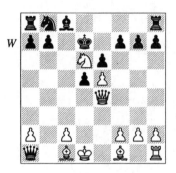

21b: after 12...♔d7

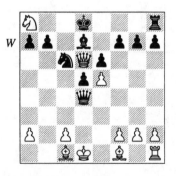

21c: after 15...♛d4+

Surprise 21   *B*

Soundness: 3   Surprise Value: 4

Sicilian: Pin with 6...♘e4

Here we consider the position after **1 e4 c5 2 ♘f3 e6 3 d4 cxd4 4 ♘xd4 ♘f6 5 ♘c3 ♗b4 6 e5 ♘e4** *(21a)*. Black's last move deviates from the standard 6...♘d5. Black's position is much tougher than it seems. The main line runs **7 ♕g4 ♕a5 8 ♕xe4 ♗xc3+ 9 bxc3 ♕xc3+ 10 ♔d1 ♕xa1 11 ♘b5 d5** and now White has a choice:

a) **12 ♘d6+ ♔d7** *(21b)* and then:

a1) **13 ♕f3 f5 14 ♘b5 ♘c6 15 ♕a3** was played in A.Martin-T.Wall, Newcastle 1996 and now 15...♖d8!.

a2) **13 ♕b4 ♘c6 14 ♗b5 ♕xe5 15 ♗a3** (Bryson-T.Wall, Newcastle 1996) 15...♖d8! is playable for Black, e.g. 16 ♖e1 ♕a1+ 17 ♔d2 ♕f6 18 ♘e8 ♔xe8 19 ♕f8+ ♔d7 20 ♕d6+ ♔e8 is a draw.

b) **12 ♕b4** (you'll find this in theory book as the refutation of Black's play) is met by 12...♘c6! (12...♘a6 loses according to old analysis by Euwe) 13 ♘c7+ ♔d8 14 ♕d6+ ♗d7 15 ♘xa8 and now, rather than **15...♕xe5** 16 ♗a3! ♕d4+ 17 ♔c1 ♕a1+ 18 ♔d2 ♕d4+ 19 ♗d3 ♕xf2+ 20 ♔d1! with a winning attack, Black must play **15...♕d4+!** *(21c)* (E.L. Stewart's idea: Black wants White to play ♗d3 so the h1-rook will hang) 16 ♗d3 ♕xe5 17 ♗f4 (17 ♕xe5 ♘xe5 and Black will pick up the a8-knight) 17...♕a1+ 18 ♗c1 (18 ♔d2 ♕xh1 and Black seems to survive – the resource ...♕b1-b4+ is useful; 18 ♔e2 ♕xh1 is also good for Black: ...♘d4+ is one annoying possibility) 18...♕e5 repeats.

Surprise 22   *B*

Soundness: 2   Surprise Value: 4

c3 Sicilian: Sherzer's line

Sherzer's ambitious but experimental idea is, after **1 e4 c5 2 c3 ♘f6 3 e5 ♘d5 4 d4**, to avoid exchanging on d4, playing instead **4...e6 5 ♘f3 ♘c6** *(22a)*. If White ignores the fact that Black has not exchanged, then he forfeits some options. **6 c4 ♘db4 7 d5 exd5** (7...♘d4 is possible) **8 cxd5 ♘d4 9 ♘xd4 cxd4** is critical:

a) **10 ♗c4?** ♕c7 wins a good pawn, since 11 ♕e2?? drops a piece.

b) **10 a3 ♕a5! 11 ♗d2 d3! 12 axb4 ♕xa1** *(22b)* doesn't seem to give White enough for the exchange:

b1) **13 ♗xd3** ♕xb2 14 0-0 ♕d4 15 ♕f3 ♗xb4 16 ♕g3 ♗xd2 17 ♘xd2 0-0 18 ♘e4 h6 19 ♘d6 g5 20 ♘f5 ♕f4 21 ♕h3 d6 ∓ Blauert-Sehner, W.German Ch 1989.

b2) **13 d6** ♕xb2 14 ♘c3 a5 15 b5 a4 16 ♕c1 ♕xc1+ 17 ♗xc1 a3 led to a winning ending in Ullrich-Nocke, 1995.

b3) **13 ♗c3** d2+! 14 ♘xd2 ♕xd1+ 15 ♔xd1 d6 16 f4 ♗g4+ 17 ♔c2 ♖c8 18 ♔b3 a6 19 ♗d3 ♖d8 20 ♗e4 ♗e7 21 ♖e1 0-0 22 f5 dxe5 23 h3 ♗h4 and Black went on to win a tough game in Lenchner-Sherzer, New York Open 1987.

c) **10 ♗e2** *(22c)* is the critical test. Then 10...♕a5 11 0-0 ♕xd5 12 ♗f3 and 10...♕c7 11 0-0 ♕xe5 12 ♖e1 are both too risky, while 10...♗c5 11 ♗f3 0-0 12 0-0 d6 13 a3 ♘a6 14 b4 ♗b6 15 ♗f4 can't be bad for White, Hingst-Jantzen, Hamburg Ch 1991.

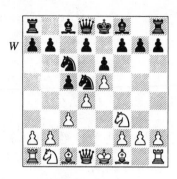

22a: after 5...♘c6

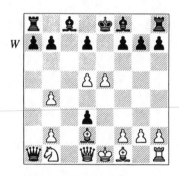

22b: after 12...♕xa1

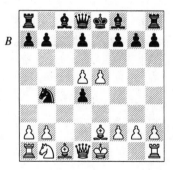

22c: after 10 ♗e2

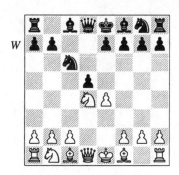

23a: after 4...d5

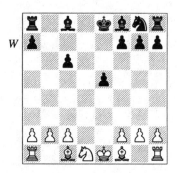

23b: after 8...e5

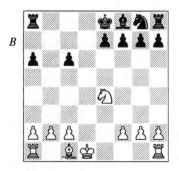

23c: after 11 ♘xe4

Surprise 23   B

Soundness: 2   Surprise Value: 4

Sicilian: 2...♘c6 and 4...d5

The position after **1 e4 c5 2 ♘f3 ♘c6 3 d4 cxd4 4 ♘xd4 d5** *(23a)* is not held in high regard in most theory manuals. However, practice is another matter, as Black has not scored too badly from here. Let's investigate:

a) **5 ♘c3** dxe4 6 ♘xc6 ♕xd1+ 7 ♔xd1 bxc6 8 ♘xe4 – compare line 'd'.

b) **5 exd5** ♕xd5 6 ♗e3 e5 7 ♘b5 ♕xd1+ 8 ♔xd1 ♗d8 9 ♗c4 ♗g4+ 10 ♔c1 ♘h5 11 f3 ♘f6 12 g4 ♗g6 13 h4 h5 14 g5 ♘d7 15 ♖d1 a6 16 ♘d6 ♗xd6 17 ♖xd6 ♔c7 18 ♖d1 ♘b6 is only a little better for White, Rogers-Armas, Wijk aan Zee 1996.

c) **5 ♘xc6 bxc6 6 exd5 ♕xd5 7 ♘c3 ♕xd1+ 8 ♘xd1 e5** *(23b)* and now:

c1) **9 ♗e2** ♗e6 10 0-0 ♘f6 11 ♗a6 ♖b8 12 ♖e1 ♗d6 13 b3 ♘d5 14 ♗b2 (Nijboer-Armas, Wijk aan Zee 1995) and now Black should play 14...f6.

c2) **9 ♘e3** f5 10 ♘c4 e4 11 ♗f4 ♘f6 12 0-0-0 ♗c5 13 ♘d6+ ♔e7 14 ♗c4 ♖d8 was OK for Black in Short-Zsu.Polgar, Monaco blindfold 1993.

d) **5 ♗b5** dxe4 6 ♘xc6 (6 0-0 ♗d7) 6...♕xd1+ 7 ♔xd1 a6 8 ♗a4 (8 ♘d4+ axb5 9 ♘xb5 ♗g4+ 10 ♔e1 0-0-0 11 ♘1c3 e5 gives Black counterplay) 8...♗d7 9 ♘c3 ♗xc6 10 ♗xc6+ bxc6 11 ♘xe4 *(23c)* and now Black's best chance appears to be 11...e5 12 ♖e1 0-0-0+ 13 ♗d2 ♗e7 14 ♖e2 ♘h6 15 ♔e1 ♘f5 16 ♗c3 f6 17 ♘d2 ♗c5 18 ♘b3 ♗b6, Magyar-Ezsöl, Hungarian Cht 1992/3, when Black actually went on to win.

Surprise 24   *B*

Soundness: 3   Surprise Value: 3

Kupreichik's 5...♗d7

This is a flexible idea: after **1 e4 c5 2 ♘f3 d6 3 d4 cxd4 4 ♘xd4 ♘f6 5 ♘c3** Black plays **5...♗d7** *(24a)*. This move keeps open various options for Black, including Dragon and Scheveningen set-ups, in either case seeking to avoid White's more dangerous systems (the Yugoslav and Keres Attacks respectively). Note that the move ...♗d7 is by no means out of place in either: there is a version of the Modern Scheveningen in which the bishop goes to d7. White can reply:

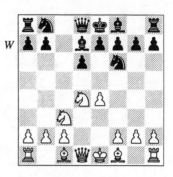

24a: after 5...♗d7

a) **6 ♗e2** can lead to sharp play:

a1) **6...g6 7 g4 h6 8 ♗e3 e5 9 ♘db5 ♗c6** *(24b)* is an interesting way to make use of the fact that there is no knight on c6, F.Cuijpers-Kupreichik, 2nd Bundesliga 1994.

a2) **6...e6 7 g4** (a kind of Keres Attack; 7 0-0 ♗e7 8 f4 ♘c6 transposes to a line of the Modern Scheveningen) **7...h6 8 f4 e5!?** *(24c)* **9 ♘f5 ♗c6 10 ♗f3 g6 11 ♘g3** (11 ♘e3 exf4 12 ♘ed5 g5) **11...♘bd7 12 f5 g5 13 a4 a6 14 ♕e2 ♗e7 15 ♗e3 b5 16 a5 ♗b7** with a reasonable game for Black, Sturua-Zviagintsev, Pula Echt 1997.

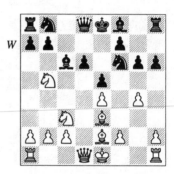

24b: after 9...♗c6

b) **6 g3 ♘c6** (6...g6 leads to a variation of the Dragon) **7 ♗g2 e6 8 0-0 a6 9 ♘xc6 ♗xc6** ½-½ Inkiov-Wojtkiewicz, Regensburg 1996.

c) **6 ♗e3 ♘g4 7 ♗g5 h6 8 ♗h4 g5 9 ♗g3 ♗g7 10 ♕d2** (10 ♗e2 ♕c8 11 ♘d5 ♘e5 12 c3 ♘bc6 13 ♘f5 ♗xf5 14 exf5 0-0 is unclear, Sulipa-Kupreichik, Groningen Open 1997) **10...♘c6 11 ♘b3 a5 12 a4 ♖c8** can't be bad for Black, Wehmeier-Atalik, Groningen Open 1997.

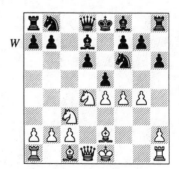

24c: after 8...e5

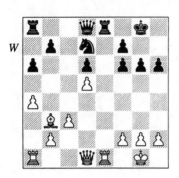

24d: after 17...exf6

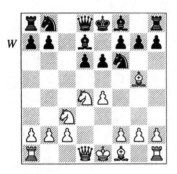

24e: after 6...e6

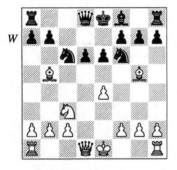

24f: after 8...♞c6

d) 6 ♗c4!? ♞c6 (this can transpose to a Sozin, Richter-Rauzer or Dragon!) 7 0-0 (7 ♗e3 ♞g4; 7 ♗g5 is a minor variation of Richter-Rauzer) 7...g6 8 ♞xc6 ♗xc6 9 ♞d5 ♗g7 10 ♗g5 ♗xd5 11 exd5 0-0 12 ♖e1 h6 13 ♗h4 a6 14 a4 ♖e8 15 c3 ♞d7 16 ♗b3 ♗f6 17 ♗xf6 exf6!? *(24d)* (otherwise it is hard for Black to find counterplay) 18 ♕d4 ♖e5 19 f4 ♖xe1+ 20 ♖xe1 b5 21 ♗d1 ♕b6 22 ♖e7 ♕xd4+ 23 cxd4 ♞b6 24 a5 ♔f8 25 ♖b7 ♞c4! is good for Black, Mortensen-Larsen, Danish Ch 1994.

e) 6 ♗g5 e6 *(24e)* (6...♞c6 transposes to a main line of the Richter-Rauzer) and then:

e1) 7 ♕d2 a6 8 f4 h6 (Black avoids transposing to a Richter-Rauzer) 9 ♗xf6 (9 ♗h4? ♞xe4) 9...♕xf6 10 0-0-0 ♞c6 with an interesting position where White's attacking chances should not be underestimated.

e2) 7 f4 ♞c6 (7...h6 seems more consistent) 8 ♞db5 ♕b8 9 e5 dxe5 10 ♗xf6 gxf6 11 ♕d2 f5 12 0-0-0 ♕d8 13 fxe5 ♞xe5 14 ♕d4 gave White dangerous attacking chances in the game Van den Doel-Kupreichik, Groningen 1996.

e3) 7 ♞db5 ♗xb5!? (7...♗c6 8 ♗xf6 gxf6 9 ♕h5 a6 10 ♞d4 ♗d7 11 0-0-0 ♞c6 12 ♞xc6 bxc6 13 ♗c4 ♕b6 14 ♖hf1 ♖b8 15 ♗b3 c5 16 ♕e2 ♗b5 17 ♞xb5 axb5 18 c4 bxc4 19 ♕xc4 is still a bit awkward for Black, whose king's long-term safety is in doubt, V.Spasov-Kupreichik, Moscow OL 1994) 8 ♗xb5+ ♞c6 *(24f)* 9 ♕f3 h6 10 ♗h4 ♗e7 11 e5 ♞d5 12 ♗xc6+ bxc6 13 ♗xe7 ♕xe7 14 ♕g3 dxe5 15 ♕xg7 ♕f6 16 ♕xf6 ♞xf6 17 0-0-0 ♞d5 led to a draw in Benjamin-Zviagintsev, Groningen FIDE Wch 1997.

Surprise 25   *W*

Soundness: 4   Surprise Value: 4

Kan: 5 ♗d3 g6 6 b3

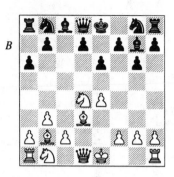

25a: after 7 ♗b2

After **1 e4 c5 2 ♘f3 e6 3 d4 cxd4 4 ♘xd4 a6 5 ♗d3**, 5...g6 looks a little odd, but if White does nothing dramatic, Black can set up an acceptable Hedgehog/Double Fianchetto position. **6 b3 ♗g7 7 ♗b2** *(25a)* seeks to frustrate that little idea:

a) **7...♘e7?** 8 ♘c6 (8 ♘xe6?? ♕a5+ would of course be most embarrassing) 8...♗xb2 (if Black allows ♗xg7, then his dark squares will be disastrously weak) 9 ♘xd8 ♗xa1 10 c3 d5 (10...♔xd8 11 ♕c1 traps the bishop, and wins) 11 ♕c1 d4 12 cxd4 ♔xd8 13 ♘c3 ♗xc3+ 14 ♕xc3 and although Black has quite a lot of material for the queen, White has a strong initiative.

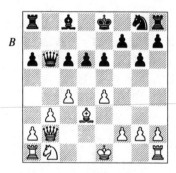

25b: after 12 ♕xb2

b) **7...♕b6** looks like a good idea, since after 8 c3 ♘c6 Black seems to have turned the tension on the long diagonal to his advantage. However, after 9 ♘xc6 bxc6 10 ♕c2! d6 11 c4 ♗xb2 12 ♕xb2 *(25b)* we see that White has really won the skirmish. Then after 12...e5 13 ♘c3 ♘e7 14 0-0 0-0 15 ♘a4 ♕c7 (Nevednichy-Badea, Bucharest 1996) Nevednichy recommends 16 c5! d5 17 ♘b6 ♖a7 18 f4! exf4 19 ♕f6 ±.

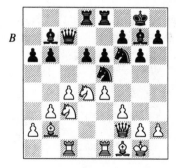

25c: after 17 ♖c1

c) **7...♘f6 8 0-0 0-0** (8...d6 would also be met by 9 ♘d2, rather than 9 c4 0-0 10 ♘c3 ♘bd7, e.g. 11 ♖e1 ♖e8 12 ♗f1 b6 13 ♕d2 ♗b7 14 ♖ad1 ♕c7 15 f3 ♖ad8 16 ♕f2 ♘e5 17 ♖c1 *(25c)* 17...d5! 18 exd5 ♘fg4! 19 ♕g3 ♘xf3+! winning, R.Byrne-Andersson, Amsterdam 1979) **9 ♘d2** *(25d)* and then:

c1) **9...♘h5?!** 10 ♖e1 (freeing f1 as a retreat-square, so ...♘f4 would now be striking at air) 10...b6 11 ♘c4 ♗b7?! (11...d6 12

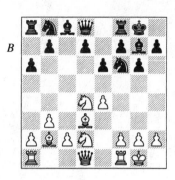

25d: after 9 ᐸd2

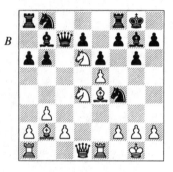

25e: after 14 ♗e4

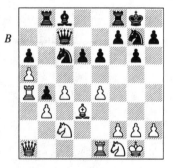

25f: after 18 ᐸf1

a4) 12 ᐸd6 ♕c7 13 e5! ᐸf4 (13...♗xe5??
14 ♖xe5 ♕xd6 15 ♕xh5! gxh5 16 ♖g5+
♔h8 17 ᐸf5+) 14 ♗e4! *(25e)* 14...♗xe4 15
♖xe4 ᐸd5 (15...♗xe5?? 16 ᐸ4b5 axb5 17
♗xe5 ᐸh5 18 ᐸxf7 threatens the queen and
ᐸh6#) 16 c4 f5 17 ♖e1 ᐸe7 18 ᐸf3 ᐸbc6
and now **19 a4!** seals Black up completely,
e.g. 19...ᐸc8 20 ♗a3. Instead after **19
♕d2?!** b5! 20 h4 bxc4 21 bxc4 ♖ab8 22
♗c3 ᐸc8! things had become unclear in
Ivanchuk-Shirov, Monte Carlo Amber rpd
1996.

c2) **9...ᐸc6** 10 ᐸxc6 dxc6 11 e5 ᐸd7
(11...ᐸd5 12 ᐸe4 looks like some lines of
the Alekhine Defence, except Black's pieces
are on the wrong squares!) 12 f4 is good for
White – Nunn.

c3) **9...d6** is probably Black's best, when
rather than going into a full Maroczy structure with **10 c4**, when Black can happily curl
up into a Hedgehog with 10...ᐸbd7 followed by ...b6, ...♗b7, etc. (e.g. 11 ♖c1 ♕c7
12 ♔h1 b6 13 f4 ♗b7 14 ♕e2 e5 15 fxe5
ᐸxe5 16 ♗b1 ♖ae8 17 ♖f4 ♕e7 with a reasonable game for Black, Fishbein-Vyzh-
manavin, Moscow 1989), I prefer Geller's
treatment: **10 ♖e1** ♕c7 11 a4 b6 12 a5 b5 13
c4 b4 14 ᐸc2 ᐸc6 15 ♖a4 ♖b8 16 ♕a1 ᐸh5
17 ♗xg7 ᐸxg7 18 ᐸf1 *(25f)* with heavy
pressure, although Black managed to survive by dogged defence after 18...♗d7 19
♗e2 ♕a7 20 ᐸfe3 h5 21 ♖d1 ♕c5 22 ♖a2
♖bd8 23 ᐸd4 ᐸe8 24 ♖ad2 ♖c8 25 ᐸxc6
♗xc6 26 ♗d3 ♖c7 27 ♗c2 ♗b7 in Geller-
Ignatiev, Kislovodsk 1968.

Surprise 26   W

Soundness: 3   Surprise Value: 3

Milner-Barry's Other Gambit

Aside from his well-known gambit in the French Defence, Sir Stuart Milner-Barry devised another interesting sacrificial continuation, which may turn out to be of more enduring value. It occurs after **1 e4 c5 2 c3 d5 3 exd5 ♕xd5 4 d4 cxd4 5 cxd4 ♘c6 6 ♘f3 e5 7 ♘c3 ♗b4** (one of the lines recommended for Black against the c3 Sicilian by Joe Gallagher in his popular book *Beating the Anti-Sicilians*). Sir Stuart's idea was, rather than the old move 8 ♗d2, to play **8 ♗e2!?** *(26a)*, planning to sacrifice a piece if Black plays the natural 8...e4, and this is discussed in the next Surprise. Otherwise White seeks to benefit from the fact that ♗e2 and 0-0 is a more constructive way to break the pin than the clumsy ♗d2. The other variations are as follows:

a) **8...exd4 9 0-0** sees Black resorting to quiet means to sue for peace:

a1) **9...♗xc3?!** 10 bxc3 ♘ge7 11 ♘xd4 *(26b)* is uncomfortable for Black: 11...♕a5 (11...0-0 12 ♘xc6 ♕xc6 13 ♗a3 ♖e8 14 ♗f3 puts Black under great pressure, Ponomariov-Savić, Zagan jr Wch 1997) 12 ♘xc6 ♘xc6 13 ♕d6 ♕e5 14 ♕xe5+ ♘xe5 15 f4 ± Liss-Sutovsky, Rishon le Zion 1995.

a2) **9...♕d8** (a sound move) 10 ♘b5 *(26c)* 10...♘f6 (10...♘ge7 11 ♘fxd4 0-0 12 ♗f4 ♘xd4 13 ♕xd4 ♕xd4 14 ♘xd4 puts pressure on Black's queenside, Rabiega-Odendahl, German Ch (Binz) 1995) and now **11 a3** planning b4 and ♗b2 seems a better try than **11 ♘bxd4** ♘xd4 12 ♕xd4 ♕xd4 13 ♘xd4 0-0 14 ♗g5 (14 ♗f3 ♖d8) 14...♘e4

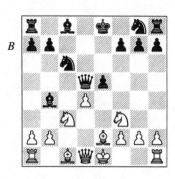

26a: after 8 ♗e2

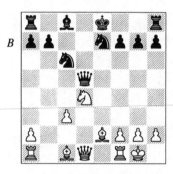

26b: after 11 ♘xd4

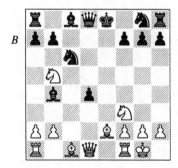

26c: after 10 ♘b5

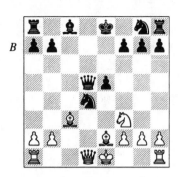

26d: after 10 ♗xc3

26e: after 16...♖f8

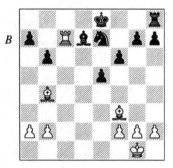

26f: after 19 ♖c7

15 ♗e3 ♗d7 16 ♗f3 ♖fe8 17 ♖ac1 ♗a5 18 ♘b3 ♗b6 19 ♗xb6 axb6 20 ♖fe1 ♘c5 21 ♖xe8+ ♖xe8 22 ♘xc5 bxc5 ½-½ Har-Zvi – Sutovsky, Tel Aviv 1995.

b) **8...♘xd4** (Gallagher's recommendation) **9 ♗d2 ♗xc3 10 ♗xc3** *(26d)* and now:

b1) **10...♘f6** allows White an edge after **11 ♘xd4** exd4 12 ♕xd4 0-0 (a move Black cannot play in the analogous position in line 'b2') 13 0-0 (N.Pedersen-Tindall, Medellin jr Wch 1996) or **11 0-0** ♘xe2+ 12 ♕xe2 0-0 13 ♖fd1 ♕e4 14 ♕xe4 ♘xe4 15 ♗xe5 ♗g4 16 ♖d5 ♖fd8 17 ♖ad1 ♖xd5 18 ♖xd5 (Acs-Sziebert, Budapest 1995) but its size should not be overestimated.

b2) **10...♘e7** 11 ♘xd4 exd4 12 ♕xd4 ♕xg2 (12...♕xd4 13 ♗xd4 ±) 13 0-0-0 ♗e6 14 ♗b5+ ♘c6 15 ♖hg1 ♕xh2 16 ♕xg7 ♖f8 *(26e)* 17 ♗xc6+ bxc6 18 ♕xf8+! won nicely in Lemmers-Van Blitterswijk, Netherlands 1995.

b3) **10...♘xf3+** 11 ♗xf3 ♕xd1+ 12 ♖xd1 f6 13 ♗a5 ♗e6 (Gallagher's improvement over Finkel's 13...♗d7 14 ♗xb7 ♖b8 15 ♗d5 ±) 14 ♖c1!? (14 ♗xb7 ♖b8 15 ♗c6+ ♔f7 followed by 16...♘e7 is enough for equality) 14...♖c8 15 0-0 b6 16 ♖xc8+ ♗xc8 17 ♖c1 ♘e7 18 ♗b4 ♗d7 19 ♖c7 *(26f)* 19...a5 20 ♗a3 ♔d8 21 ♖b7 ♘c8 22 ♗d5 (keeping Black tied up) 22...♖e8 23 f3 g5 24 g4 ♖h8 25 b3 h5 26 h3 h4 27 ♗e4 ♖g8 28 ♔f2 ♖g7 29 ♔e3 ♖f7 30 ♗f5 ♖g7 31 ♗f8 ♖f7 32 ♔d2 b5 33 ♗c5 b4 34 ♗g6 ♖g7 35 ♗e4 ♖g8 36 ♖b8 ♔c7 37 ♖b7+ ♔d8 38 ♔e3 ♖e8 39 ♗f5 ♗xf5 40 gxf5 e4 41 fxe4 ♖h8 42 ♔f3 ♖h6 43 ♗f8 1-0 Acs-Fang, Budapest 1996.

Surprise 27   W

Soundness: 4   Surprise Value: 3

Milner-Barry: 8...e4 9 0-0

After **1 e4 c5 2 c3 d5 3 exd5 ♕xd5 4 d4 cxd4 5 cxd4 ♘c6 6 ♘f3 e5 7 ♘c3 ♗b4 8 ♗e2 e4**, White sacrifices a piece by **9 0-0!** **♗xc3 10 bxc3 exf3 11 ♗xf3** *(27a)*. Black's defence is difficult:

a) **11...♕a5** 12 ♖e1+ ♘ge7 13 d5 0-0 14 c4 ♖d8 15 ♕e2 ♘d4 16 ♕xe7 ♗d7 17 ♗h5 g6 18 ♗e3 ♘c2 19 ♖f1 ♖e8 (19...♘xa1 20 ♕f6 ♘c2 21 ♗h6 +–) 20 ♕xd7 ♘xa1 21 ♖xa1 ♕c3 22 ♖d1 ♕c2 23 ♕xb7 gxh5 24 ♕b3 ± Rõtšagov-G.Mohr, Moscow 1994.

b) **11...♕c4** 12 ♖e1+ ♗e6 13 d5 0-0-0 loses to the thematic queen sacrifice 14 dxc6! ♖xd1 15 cxb7+, Muniz-Shtanchaev, Roque Saenz Pena U-26 Wcht 1997.

c) **11...♕d6** 12 ♖e1+ ♘ce7 13 a4 ♔f8 14 ♗a3 ♕f6 15 ♖e3 *(27b)* and White piles up on e7, Trabert-Donk, Groningen 1996.

d) **11...♕f5** 12 ♗a3!? (12 ♖e1+ ♗e6 13 d5 0-0-0 14 c4 ♘f6 15 ♗b2 ♔b8 16 ♕b3 ♘xd5 17 cxd5 ♗xd5 18 ♗xd5 ♕xd5 19 ♕xd5 ♖xd5 20 ♗xg7 ♖hd8 only gave White a slight advantage in Rosandić-Trauth, Cannes 1995) 12...♘ge7 (12...♗e6 13 ♖b1) 13 ♖e1 ♗e6 14 d5 0-0-0 *(27c)* 15 dxc6!! ♖xd1 (15...♘xc6 16 ♕a4 ♗d5 17 ♗g4) 16 cxb7+ ♔c7 17 ♖axd1 ♘c8 (17...♘c6 18 ♗d6+ ♔xb7 19 ♖b1+ ♔a6 20 ♗xc6) 18 c4! ♕f4 (White also wins after 18...♕a5 19 ♗b2 ♘d6 20 ♗e5 or 18...f6!? 19 bxc8♕+ ♔xc8 20 ♖d6 ♗d7 21 ♖d5) 19 ♗b2! ♘d6 20 ♗e5 ♕xe5 21 ♖xe5 winning, Motylev-Malakhov, Russian U-20 Ch 1996.

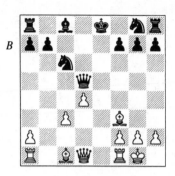

27a: after 11 ♗xf3

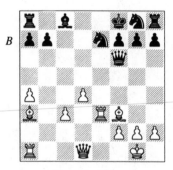

27b: after 15 ♖e3

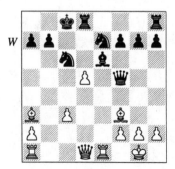

27c: after 14...0-0-0

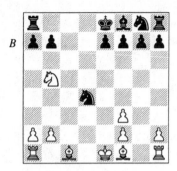

28a: after 10 ♘b5

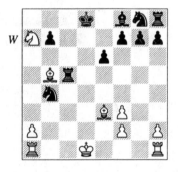

28b: after 15...e6

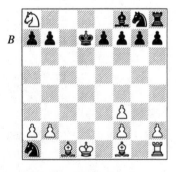

28c: after 13 ♘xa8

Surprise 28   B

Soundness: 2   Surprise Value: 4

c3 Sicilian: unrefuted line

The position after **1 e4 c5 2 c3 d5 3 exd5 ♕xd5 4 d4 cxd4 5 cxd4 ♘c6 6 ♘f3 ♗g4 7 ♘c3 ♗xf3 8 gxf3 ♕xd4 9 ♕xd4 ♘xd4 10 ♘b5** *(28a)* has for many years been regarded as a disaster for Black. Indeed, White has scored very heavily from this position in practice, but it should be noted that in many of these games Black reached diagram 28a purely by accident – the moves leading to it are very natural. Here we consider three main attempts by Black to hold his position together.

A few comments on move-order:

1) White can avoid the issue by playing 7 ♗e2, leading to a normal line, but this rules out certain options that White has in the standard variations where Black does not play an early ...cxd4. Besides, most players will be delighted to play 7 ♘c3.

2) The position could be reached via a Morra Gambit move-order, in which Black will have already played ...cxd4.

3) If diagram 28a is playable for Black, then in the Panov Attack (1 e4 c6 2 d4 d5 3 exd5 cxd5 4 c4), he could try 4...♘c6, since then 5 cxd5 ♕xd5 transposes to our line of the Sicilian.

Black's defensive tries all start with **10...♘c2+ 11 ♔d1**:

a) **11...♖c8** 12 ♘xa7 ♖c5 13 b4 (13 ♗e3 ♘xe3+ 14 fxe3 is level) 13...♘xb4 14 ♗b5+ ♔d8! 15 ♗e3 e6! *(28b)* 16 ♗a4 (16 ♗xc5 ♗xc5 wins the a7-knight) 16...♘f6! 17 ♗xc5 ♗xc5 (Black has at least enough compensation) 18 ♘b5 ♔e7 19 ♔e2 ♘fd5 20

♖hd1 h5 21 ♖ac1 b6 22 a3 ♘f4+ 23 ♔f1 ♘bd5 24 ♗b3 h4 25 a4 ♖a8 26 ♘c3 ♘xc3 27 ♖xc3 g5 28 ♖c2 ♖a7 29 ♖cd2 ½-½ Mes-van der Meiden, corr. 1991.

b) **11...♘xa1 12 ♘c7+ ♔d7 13 ♘xa8** *(28c)* and now:

b1) **13...g6** 14 ♗e3 (14 ♗f4 ♗h6 15 ♗e5 f6 16 ♗b5+ ♔c8 17 ♗d4 ♔b8 18 ♘b6 axb6 19 ♗xb6 e5 20 ♗e3 ♗xe3 21 fxe3 ♘e7 22 ♗a4 ♖c8 23 ♔d2 ♖c4 24 ♗d1 ♘c6 25 b3 ♖c5 0-1 Gluck-Pastorini, Parigi 1989) 14...♗h6 15 ♗b5+ ♔d6 16 ♗xa7 ♘f6 17 ♘b6 ♖d8 18 ♔e2 ♘c2 19 ♖d1+ ♔c7 20 ♖xd8 ♔xd8 21 ♘c4 ♗f4 22 a3! *(28d)* 22...e5?! (22...♗xh2?! 23 ♗a4; 22...♘d5 23 ♗a4; 22...♗b8) 23 h3 ♘d5 24 ♗a4 ♘d4+ 25 ♗xd4 exd4 26 ♔d3 and White won a pawn in Crouch-Balinas, London 1979.

28d: after 22 a3

b2) **13...♔c6** *(28e)* and then:

b21) **14 b4** e6 15 b5+ (15 ♗b2 ♘f6) 15...♔d7 16 ♗b2 ♘f6 17 ♖g1 (17 ♗xa1 ♗e7 18 ♖g1 g6) 17...♗b4 18 ♖xg7 ♔e7 *(28f)* should boil down to an ending where Black, at least, will be in no danger.

b22) **14 ♗f4** e6 15 ♗d3 (15 ♘c7 ♘f6 16 ♗b5+ ♔b6 17 ♔d2 ♗b4+ 18 ♔d3 ♖d8+ 19 ♔c4 ♘c2 and the dance of the pieces ends in Black's favour) 15...♗d6 (15...♘f6 is possible too, since after 16 ♘c7 ♘h5 White's pieces are hanging) 16 ♗e4+ ♔d7 17 ♗g5 (17 ♗xd6 ♔xd6 18 ♗xb7 ♘f6 leaves White's pieces in trouble) 17...♘f6 (17...h6 is more ambitious) 18 ♗xf6 gxf6 19 ♔e2 ♖xa8 20 ♖xa1 f5 21 ♗d3 h6 ½-½ (Black should of course play on here) Heppe-kausen-Hubbertz, Aachen 1993.

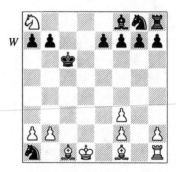

28e: after 13...♔c6

b23) **14 ♗g2** ♘f6 15 f4+ ♘d5 16 ♘c7! ♔xc7 17 ♗xd5 g6 18 ♗e3 ♗g7 17 ♔c1 and the knight is still in trouble.

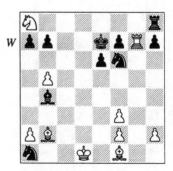

28f: after 18...♔e7

29a: after 8...g5

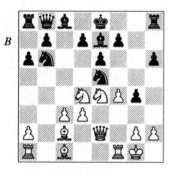

29b: after 18 f2-f4

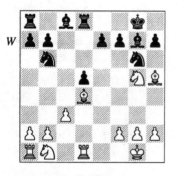

29c: after 17...♘g6

Surprise 29   *B*

Soundness: 4   Surprise Value: 2

c3 Sicilian: 7...♕c7 8 ♕e2 g5

In recent years **1 e4 c5 2 c3 ♘f6 3 e5 ♘d5 4 ♘f3** (rather than the more forcing 4 d4 cxd4 5 ♘f3) **4...♘c6 5 ♗c4 ♘b6 6 ♗b3** has been proving annoying for Black. The fact that White has held back with his d-pawn gives him plenty of flexibility, which shows up to his advantage in such lines as 6...d5 7 exd6 ♕xd6 8 ♘a3!? and 6...c4 7 ♗c2 g6 (7...d6 8 exd6 ♕xd6 9 ♘a3) 8 b3! d5 9 exd6 ♕xd6 10 0-0 ♗g7 11 ♘a3.

Ivanchuk's idea **6...c4 7 ♗c2 ♕c7 8 ♕e2 g5!?** *(29a)* has therefore attracted attention. The need for such a dramatic move is shown by 8...g6 9 d4!? cxd3 10 ♗xd3 ♗g7 11 ♗f4 and 8...e6 9 b3 g5 10 ♘a3 g4 11 ♘b5 ♕b8 12 ♘g5 ♘xe5 13 bxc4 a6 14 ♘d4 ♘bxc4 15 0-0 h6 16 ♘e4 ♗e7 17 d3 ♘b6 18 f4 *(29b)*, when Black's position is loose, Kuijf-Stripunsky, Wijk aan Zee 1996.

White may reply:

a) **9 h3 ♗g7** puts the heat on e5.

b) **9 ♘xg5 ♕xe5 10 d4** (White gets nowhere with 10 ♕xe5 ♘xe5 11 ♘xh7? ♗h6 trapping the knight, 10 ♘xh7?! ♗h6 11 ♘a3 ♗g7 or 10 ♘f3 ♕xe2+ 11 ♔xe2 ♗g7 12 d4 cxd3+ 13 ♗xd3 d5 ∓) 10...cxd3 11 ♗xd3 ♕xe2+ 12 ♗xe2 ♗g7 (12...h6 only helps White regroup) 13 0-0 0-0 14 ♖d1 d5 15 ♗e3 ♖d8 16 ♗h5!? (16 ♘a3 ♘a4) 16...♘e5! 17 ♗d4 ♘g6! *(29c)* gave Black an excellent position in Torre-Ivanchuk, Erevan OL 1996, from which he went on to win.

c) White's 'counter-surprise' is discussed next.

Surprise 30   **W**

Soundness: 3   Surprise Value: 3

Ivanchuk's 8...g5: 9 e6!?

From what we have just seen, **1 e4 c5 2 c3 ♘f6 3 e5 ♘d5 4 ♘f3 ♘c6 5 ♗c4 ♘b6 6 ♗b3 c4 7 ♗c2 ♕c7 8 ♕e2 g5!?** appears quite safe and sound. However, White has the reply **9 e6!? dxe6 10 ♘xg5** *(30a)*, damaging Black's pawn structure. Black must seek piece activity to compensate, but first he must take the queens off by **10...♕e5!** (10...h6 11 ♘f3 ♗g7 12 0-0 0-0 13 ♘a3 gives White attacking chances). Then:

a) **11 ♘xh7? ♗h6** traps the knight.

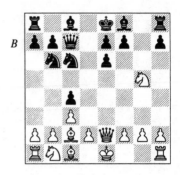

30a: after 10 ♘xg5

b) **11 d4** cxd3 12 ♗xd3 ♕xe2+ 13 ♗xe2 (13 ♔xe2 f5!) 13...h6 14 ♘e4 e5 15 ♘a3 ♗f5 *(30b)* 16 ♘g3 (16 ♗f3 0-0-0 17 ♘c2 e6 18 ♗d2 ♗g6 19 0-0-0 f5 20 ♘g3 e4 and Black hung on in Rozentalis-Hellers, Århus 1997) 16...♗g6 17 ♘c4 ♘d5 18 0-0 0-0-0 19 ♖e1 h5 20 h4 e6 21 ♗f3 f6 22 a4 ♔c7 23 a5 ♗d3 24 ♖a4 ♗c5 25 ♗e4 ♗xe4 26 ♘xe4 ♗e7 27 ♗d2 ♖hg8 28 b4 a6 29 ♖b1 f5 is messy and quite good for Black, Adams-Svidler, Groningen FIDE Wch 1997.

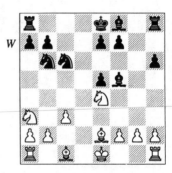

30b: after 15...♗f5

c) **11 ♘e4 f5 12 ♘g3 ♗h6** (12...♕xe2+ 13 ♘xe2 ♗g7 14 ♘a3 0-0 15 0-0 ♗d7 16 ♖b1 ♖ac8 17 b3 cxb3 18 axb3 e5 19 f3 a5 20 ♖e1 ± Sveshnikov-Sakaev, St Petersburg Chigorin mem 1997) 13 ♘a3 ♕xe2+ (13...0-0 14 d4) 14 ♔xe2 0-0 *(30c)* and now **15 d3!?** ♗xc1 16 ♖axc1 cxd3+ 17 ♗xd3 e5 18 ♖hd1 might offer White an edge. Instead **15 b3** cxb3 16 ♗xb3 ♘d5 17 ♖e1 ♘f4+ 18 ♔f1 ♘d3! gave Black counterplay in Sveshnikov-Cherniaev, Erevan Open 1996.

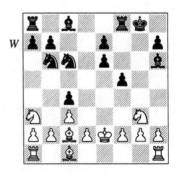

30c: after 14...0-0

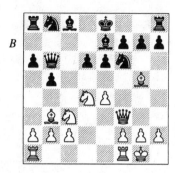

31a: after 10 ♗g5

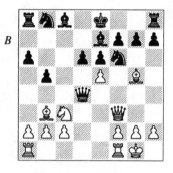

31b: after 11 e5

31c: after 13...♘xd6

Surprise 31   W

Soundness: 3   Surprise Value: 4

Najdorf-Sozin: 10 ♗g5!?

After **1 e4 c5 2 ♘f3 d6 3 d4 cxd4 4 ♘xd4 ♘f6 5 ♘c3 a6 6 ♗c4 e6 7 0-0 b5 8 ♗b3 ♗e7 9 ♕f3 ♕b6**, a position which can occur from both the Najdorf and Scheveningen, White normally plays 10 ♗e3. However, there turns out to be the interesting alternative **10 ♗g5!?** *(31a)*, since taking the knight runs into some tactics. This is still almost unexplored, despite its use in 1996 by Ivanchuk. Some analysis:

a) **10...b4** 11 e5! ♗b7 12 ♘a4 ♕c7 13 exd6 ♗xd6 14 ♕h3 should be quite good for White.

b) **10...♕xd4 11 e5** *(31b)* and then:

b1) **11...♕xe5** 12 ♗xf6 gxf6 13 ♕xa8 d5 allows 14 ♗xd5!, e.g. 14...b4 15 ♗c6+ ♔f8 16 ♘d1.

b2) **11...♘d5** 12 ♘xd5 exd5 13 ♗e3 ♕xe5 14 ♕xd5 ♕xd5 15 ♗xd5 wins the exchange.

b3) **11...♘e4** 12 ♗xe7 ♗b7 13 exd6 ♘xd6 *(31c)* 14 ♗d5!! destroys the communication between the black pieces.

b4) **11...d5** 12 exf6 gxf6 (12...♗xf6 13 ♖ad1 ♕c5 14 ♗xf6 gxf6 15 ♖fe1 gives White a pulverizing attack) 13 ♗e3 ♕e5 14 ♘xd5! exd5 15 ♕xd5 and White again wins the exchange by trapping the enemy rook in the corner.

c) **10...0-0 11 ♖ad1** and then:

c1) **11...♘bd7** 12 ♕g3 ♘c5 13 ♗h6 (13 ♖fe1 – compare 'c2') 13...♘e8 14 ♗d5 exd5 15 ♘xd5 ♕d8 16 ♘c6 ♗h4 17 ♘de7+ ♕xe7 18 ♘xe7+ ♗xe7 doesn't look enough for a queen, though White got his queen trapped a few moves later in Brooks-Browne, USA 1982.

c2) **11...♗b7** 12 ♖fe1 ♘bd7 13 ♕g3 is a fairly standard type of position, in which White has developed his pieces to more active squares than normal, but Black's queen has not been kicked away from b6.

c3) **11...b4** 12 ♘a4 ♕b7 13 c3 a5 14 c4 ♘bd7 15 ♘b5 ♕b8 16 ♕e2 ♗b7 17 f3 ♗c6 18 ♘d4 ♖c8 19 ♖d2 h6 20 ♗h4 ♘e5 21 ♘xc6 ♖xc6 22 f4 ♘g6 23 ♗g3 ♕c7 24 f5 ♘e5 25 fxe6 fxe6 26 ♗xe5 dxe5 27 c5 *(31d)* activated White's pieces nicely in Emms-Van den Doel, Port Erin 1997.

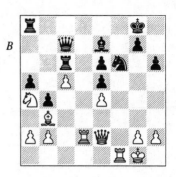

31d: after 27 c5

d) **10...♘bd7 11 ♖ad1** *(31e)* and then:

d1) **11...0-0** is line 'c1'.

d2) **11...♗b7** 12 ♖fe1 (12 ♗xe6 fxe6 13 ♘xe6 ♘e5 14 ♕h3 ♔f7 15 ♗e3 ♕c6 is unclear – Nunn) 12...♘c5 13 ♕g3 0-0-0 14 ♗e3 (threatening the g7-pawn, and preparing to sacrifice on e6) 14...g5 15 ♗xe6+ fxe6 16 ♘xe6 ♖d7 (16...♕c6 allows White to win material, while his control of d5 should stamp out counterplay) 17 b4 ♗xe4 18 bxc5 dxc5 19 ♖xd7 winning, Jaracz-Smirin, Groningen 1996.

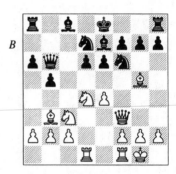

31e: after 11 ♖ad1

d3) **11...♘c5?!** 12 ♗xf6 gxf6 *(31f)* (Ivanchuk-Kamsky, Monte Carlo Amber rpd 1996) and now Nunn recommends 13 e5! ♗b7 14 ♘d5! exd5 15 exf6 ♗f8 16 ♖fe1+ ♔d8 (16...♘e4 17 ♕f5) 17 ♗xd5 ♖c8 18 ♘f5 ♗xd5 19 ♕xd5 as very good for White, e.g. 19...♕c7 20 ♖e7! ♗xe7 21 fxe7+, with a massacre.

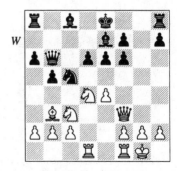

31f: after 12...gxf6

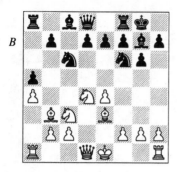

32a: after 9 a4

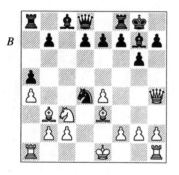

32b: after 11 ♕h4

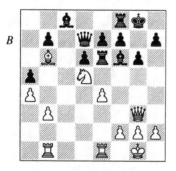

32c: after 18 ♕g3

Surprise 32   *W*

Soundness: 4   Surprise Value: 2

Uogele: 9 a4 and 11 ♕h4

White's best reply to the Accelerated Dragon, **1 e4 c5 2 ♘f3 ♘c6 3 d4 cxd4 4 ♘xd4 g6**, is undoubtedly the Maroczy Bind, 5 c4. However, for those who find that too boring, **5 ♘c3 ♗g7 6 ♗e3 ♘f6 7 ♗c4** can be recommended. Then if Black wishes to avoid transposition to a Yugoslav Attack, his main options are 7...♕a5 and Uogele's **7...0-0 8 ♗b3 a5** (8...♘g4 9 ♕xg4 ♘xd4 should here be answered by 10 ♕d1 ♘xb3 11 axb3 b6 12 ♗d4, giving Black a miserable game), when **9 a4** *(32a)* (9 f3 d5! works well for Black) has been giving Black some problems, as **9...♘g4** (9...d5 is less effective without White's dark squares weakened and with ...a4 ruled out) **10 ♕xg4 ♘xd4 11 ♕h4** *(32b)* gives White excellent attacking prospects: **11...♘xb3** (11...d6 12 ♘d5 e6 13 ♘e7+! ♔h8 14 0-0-0; 11...e6 12 ♗g5) **12 cxb3 ♖a6** (12...♗f6 13 ♕g3 d6 14 ♘d5! and the invasion on b6 and possibly a rook coming to c7 cause problems; 12...d6?! 13 ♘d5) **13 0-0 ♖e6** (13...d6 14 ♘d5) **14 ♖fe1** is the most accurate way for White to arrange his rooks:

a) **14...b6** 15 ♗h6 ♗b7 16 ♗xg7 ♔xg7 17 ♖e3 and in view of White's crude but unpleasant threats, Black felt obliged to loosen his position by 17...f5 in Topalov-Larsen, Mesa 1992.

b) **14...d6** 15 ♘d5! ♗xb2 16 ♗b6 ♕d7 17 ♖ab1 ♗f6 18 ♕g3 *(32c)* 18...♖e5 19 ♗xa5 ♕e6 20 ♗c3 led to a convincing win for White in Emms-Rausis, Gausdal Peer Gynt 1995.

Surprise 33   *W*

Soundness: 4   Surprise Value: 2

c3 Sicilian: 5...♗g4 6 dxc5

One of Black's most dependable lines of the
c3 Sicilian is **1 e4 c5 2 c3 d5 3 exd5 ♕xd5 4
d4 ♘f6 5 ♘f3 ♗g4**. Recently **6 dxc5** *(33a)*
has been used as a way to create some im-
balance. After **6...♕xc5** (for 6...♕xd1+ see
the next Surprise) **7 h3 ♗h5** (7...♗d7 8 ♘a3
e6 9 ♗e3 ♕a5 10 ♘c4 ♕c7 11 ♘ce5 ♗d6
12 ♘xd7 ♘bxd7 13 ♗b5 ± Shaked-J.Pol-
gar, Tilburg 1997; 7...♗xf3 8 ♕xf3 ±) **8
♘a3** White argues that the bishop is misplaced on g4:

a) **8...♘bd7** 9 ♗e3 ♕c8 (9...♕c7 10 ♕a4
intending ♘b5 and 0-0-0 gives White good
attacking chances) 10 ♘c4! ♕c7 (10...♗xf3
11 ♕xf3 g6 ±) 11 ♕a4! (planning ♘b6)
11...♗xf3 12 gxf3 a6 13 ♘b6 ♖d8 14 0-0-0
e6 15 ♖g1 g6 16 ♘xd7 ♖xd7 17 ♖xd7 ♕xd7
18 ♕f4 ♗e7 19 ♗d4 ♕d8 *(33b)* 20 ♗xa6!
bxa6 21 ♗xf6 ♗xf6 22 ♖d1 +– Mago-
medov-Adla, Cappelle la Grande 1997.

b) **8...a6 9 ♗e3 ♕c7 10 ♕a4+ ♘bd7 11
0-0-0** *(33c)* and then:

b1) **11...e6** 12 g4 ♗g6 13 ♗f4 (13 ♗g2
♗e4 14 ♘b5 ♕b8 15 ♘a7 ♖xa7 16 ♗xa7
♕xa7 17 ♖xd7 ♘xd7 18 ♕xe4 ♗c5 is OK
for Black, Rozentalis-Lerner, Groningen
FIDE Wch 1997) 13...♕c8 14 ♘e5 b5 15
♕a5 is possibly a bit better for White,
Cherniaev-Shipov, St Petersburg Chigorin
mem 1997.

b2) **11...♗xf3** 12 gxf3 ♖d8 13 ♘c4 e6
14 ♗b6 ♕f4+ 15 ♔b1 ♖c8 16 ♖d4 ♕b8 17
f4 ♘d5 18 ♖xd5 exd5 19 ♘e5 with good
compensation, Degraeve-Relange, French
Ch (Narbonne) 1997.

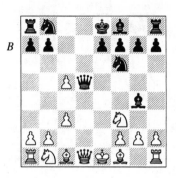

33a: after 6 dxc5

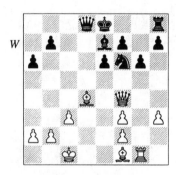

33b: after 19...♕d8

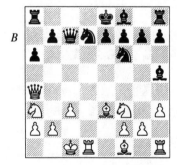

33c: after 11 0-0-0

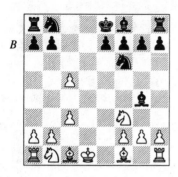

34a: after 7 ⊗xd1

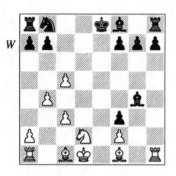

34b: after 12...exf3

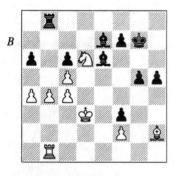

34c: after 25 ⊒b1

Surprise 34   W

Soundness: 3   Surprise Value: 4

c3: 5...♗g4 6 dxc5 ♕xd1+

We have just seen Black struggling to equalize when he keep the queens on after **1 e4 c5 2 c3 d5 3 exd5 ♕xd5 4 d4 ♘f6 5 ♘f3 ♗g4 6 dxc5**. The surprise awaiting Black if he attempts to make tactical use of the bishop's position on g4 after the queen exchange on d1 is a transition to messy, unclear ending with much in common with the Botvinnik System, viz. **6...♕xd1+ 7 ♔xd1** *(34a)* **7...e5 8 b4 e4** (8...♘c6 9 ♔c2 ♘d5 10 ♗b5 f6 11 ♔b2! ♗e7 12 ♗e3 ♗xf3 13 gxf3 a5 14 a3 0-0-0 15 ♖g1 g6 16 ♔c2 f5 17 ♗xc6 bxc6, Khmelnitsky-Christiansen, USA Ch (Parsippany) 1996, 18 c4 ♘xe3+ 19 fxe3 ±) **9 h3 ♗h5 10 g4 ♘xg4 11 hxg4 ♗xg4 12 ♘bd2 exf3** *(34b)*. Both sides have winning chances, but White's position is perhaps a little easier to play:

a) **13 ♗b5+ ♘c6 14 ♖e1+ ♗e7 15 ♔c2 ♔f8 16 ♗xc6 bxc6 17 ♘c4 h5 18 ♗f4 g5 19 ♗h2 ♖h6 20 a4 ♖e6 21 ♘d6 a6 22 ♔d3 ♔g7 23 c4 ♖b8 24 ♖xe6 ♗xe6 25 ♖b1** *(34c)* **25...♗xd6 26 ♗xd6 ♖e8 27 ♖g1 g4 28 b5 ♗f5+ 29 ♔c3 axb5 30 cxb5 cxb5 31 axb5 ♖e2 32 ♗g3** and White's pawns run through, A.Arnason-J.Arnason, Westmann Isles 1985.

b) **13 ♗d3 ♘c6 14 ♖e1+ ♗e7 15 ♔c2 a6 16 ♗e4 ♖c8 17 a4 h5 18 ♗a3 ♖h6 19 ♘xf3 ♖f6 20 ♖e3 ♖f4 21 ♗d5 ♖d8 22 ♗xc6+ bxc6 23 ♘d4 ♖xf2+ 24 ♔b3 ♗e6+? 25 ♘xe6 fxe6 26 ♖xe6 ♔f7 27 ♖xc6** and again the white pawns will touch down first, Relange-Nunn, Hastings 1997/8.

Surprise 35   *B*

Soundness: 5   Surprise Value: 2

Caro-Kann: Gunderam

I have decided to cite a convincing variation against the Gunderam line, **1 e4 c6 2 d4 d5 3 exd5 cxd5 4 c4 ♘f6 5 c5?!**, since, although well-known to many Caro-Kann players, I don't believe the analysis has appeared in print before. Some people persist in playing the Gunderam, perhaps through reading an old copy of *An Opening Repertoire for the Attacking Player*. After the best move **5...e5!** *(35a)*, Gunderam's analysis is based on a large dose of wishful thinking:

a) **6 dxe5 ♘e4 7 b4 a5** *(35b)* smashes up White's pawns.

b) **6 ♘c3 exd4 7 ♕xd4 ♘c6 8 ♗b5** is Gunderam's analysis. He continued with the absurd **8...♗d7?**, whereupon White exchanged on c6, and Black had problems coordinating his counterplay. However, Black can break the pin in a far more convenient way a move later: **8...♗e7!** 9 ♘ge2 (9 ♗xc6+ bxc6 10 ♘ge2 0-0 is the same) 9...0-0 10 ♗xc6 bxc6 11 0-0 ♘d7 ∓ *(35c)* and now we see Black has gained much more than a tempo by not playing ...♗d7. His knight can use d7, and the bishop can take up a fine post on a6. One example: 12 b4 ♗f6 13 ♕d2 a5 14 ♗a3 (14 b5 ♘xc5 15 ♗a3 d4 16 ♗xc5 dxc3) 14...♘e5 15 ♖fd1 (15 ♖ad1 ♗a6) 15...♗g4 16 ♕c1 ♖e8 17 f3 ♘xf3+! 18 gxf3 ♗xf3 19 ♕d2 ♕d7 20 ♘g3 ♕h3 0-1 (21 ♕f2 ♖e1+ is reminiscent of a famous line from Byrne-Fischer, USA Ch 1962/3) Hemming-S.Williams, corr. 1994.

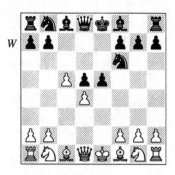

35a: after 5...e5

35b: after 7...a5

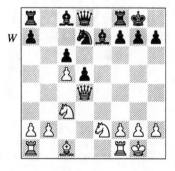

35c: after 11...♘d7

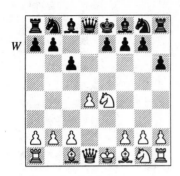

36a: after 4...h6

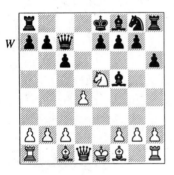

36b: after 8...♕c7

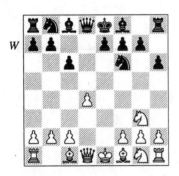

36c: after 5...♘f6

Surprise 36   *B*

Soundness: 2   Surprise Value: 4

Caro-Kann: 4...h6

After **1 e4 c6 2 d4 d5 3 ♘c3 dxe4 4 ♘xe4**
Black can try the very unusual **4...h6** *(36a)*.
The plan is 5...♗f5 6 ♘g3 ♗h7, denying
White the possibility of playing h4-h5 or
♘e2-f4 with tempo, as in the line 4...♗f5 5
♘g3 ♗g6. It is hard for White to profit from
the slowness of Black's plan:

a) **5 ♘f3 ♗f5** and then:

a1) **6 ♘c5!? ♘d7** (6...b6 7 ♗d3) 7 ♘xd7
♕xd7 8 ♘e5 ♕c7!? *(36b)* 9 ♗f4 g5 10 ♗g3
(10 ♘xf7?! ♕xf4 11 ♘xh8 ♗g7 12 ♕h5+
♔d7 13 ♘f7 ♗g4 14 ♕g6 ♗xd4 15 f3 ♗f5
16 ♕h5 ♗xc2 −+) 10...e6 is OK for Black
(11 ♘g6?? ♕a5+).

a2) **6 ♘g3 ♗h7 7 ♗d3 ♗xd3 8 ♕xd3 e6**
9 ♗d2 ♘f6 10 ♘e5 ♘bd7 11 f4 c5 is also
OK for Black, Raaste-Pyhälä, Espoo 1986.

b) **5 ♗c4 ♗f5 6 ♘g3** (6 ♕e2 ♕xd4)
6...♗h7 7 ♘1e2 ♘f6 8 0-0 e6 9 ♘f4 ♗d6 10
c3 0-0 11 ♖e1 ♖e8 12 ♘fh5 ♘bd7 13 ♕f3
♘xh5 14 ♘xh5 ♗g6 15 ♘f4 ♗f5 16 ♗d2
c5 with enough activity, Romero-Bellon,
Tarrasa 1989.

c) **5 c3 ♗f5 6 ♘g3 ♗h7 7 ♘f3 e6 8 ♗c4**
♘f6 9 0-0 ♗d6 10 ♕e2 0-0 11 ♘e5 ♕c7 12
f4 c5 13 ♗e3 is playable for Black, Fran-
zoni-Bellon, Biel 1988.

d) **5 ♘g3 ♘f6** *(36c)* and now:

d1) **6 c3 e6 7 ♘f3 c5 8 ♗d3 cxd4 9**
♘xd4 ♘bd7 10 ♕e2 ♗e7?? (10...♘c5 11
♗c2 ±) 11 ♘xe6! 1-0 Gullaksen-Egeli, Norwegian Cht (Gausdal) 1994.

d2) **6 ♘f3 e6 7 ♗d3 c5 8 dxc5 ♗xc5 9**
0-0 ♘c6 10 a3 0-0 11 b4 ♗e7 12 ♗b2 b6 =
Gullaksen-Egeli, Norwegian Ch 1995.

Surprise 37　W

Soundness: 3　Surprise Value: 3

Caro-Kann: 3 ♕f3

1 e4 c6 2 ♘c3 d5 3 ♕f3 *(37a)* is an interesting, but strangely unpopular line against the Caro-Kann. There are plenty of traps for Black, and no clear route to safe equality. The next surprise covers 3...dxe4. Here is a taster of the other main lines:

a) **3...d4 4 ♗c4!** ♘f6 5 e5 dxc3 6 exf6 cxd2+ 7 ♗xd2 exf6 8 0-0-0 with dangerous play for the pawn.

b) **3...e6 4 d4** (4 ♘h3 ♘d7 5 exd5 cxd5 6 d4 ♘gf6 7 g4 ♗b4 8 ♗d2 ♘b8?! 9 0-0-0 ♘c6 10 ♗f4 a6 11 g5 ♘d7 12 a3 ♗e7 13 ♕g3 with attacking prospects, Galego-Morović, Erevan OL 1996) 4...dxe4 (4...♘f6 5 ♗g5 ♗e7 6 e5 ♘fd7 7 ♗xe7 ♕xe7 8 ♕g3 0-0 9 f4 c5 10 ♘f3 cxd4 11 ♘xd4 ♘c6 12 0-0-0 ± f6?? 13 ♘xd5! +− Arapović-Campora, Mendrisio 1988) 5 ♘xe4 ♕xd4 6 ♗d3 *(37b)* 6...f5 7 ♘c3 ♘f6 8 ♕e2 ♗b4 9 ♗d2 0-0 10 a3 ♗d6 11 ♘f3 ♕g4 12 h3 ♕h5 13 0-0-0 with good compensation, Skuinia-Skripchenko, Manila wom OL 1992.

c) **3...♘f6 4 e5** ♘fd7 5 d4 (5 ♕g3 was played by Smyslov) 5...e6 6 ♘h3 a6 (6...h6 7 ♗e3 a6 8 ♘f4 c5 9 ♕h5 ♘b6 10 dxc5 d4 11 0-0-0 ♘c6 12 cxb6 1-0 J.Berry-Bjel, corr. 1977) 7 ♘g5 ♕e7 8 ♗d3 c5 9 ♘e2 cxd4 10 ♕g3 f6 11 ♘f3 ♘xe5 12 ♘xe5 fxe5 13 ♗xh7 ♘c6 14 0-0 ♔d7 15 ♗g6 ♕f6 16 f4 e4 17 f5 ♗d6 18 ♗f4 ♗e5 (18...e5 19 ♗g5 ♕f8 20 f6 *(37c)* wins, despite Black's beautiful pawn-centre!) 19 fxe6+ ♕xe6 20 ♗f7! ± Galego-Izeta, Seville 1992.

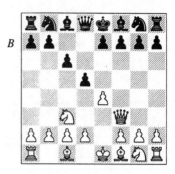

37a: after 3 ♕f3

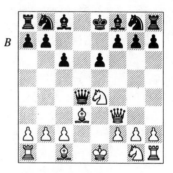

37b: after 6 ♗d3

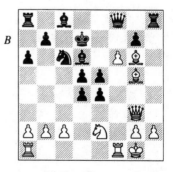

37c: after 20 f6

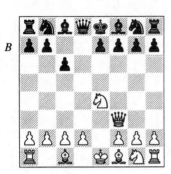

38a: after 4 ♘xe4

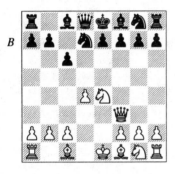

38b: after 5 d4

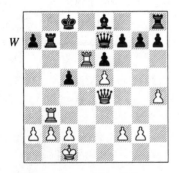

38c: after 19...♖xb7

Surprise 38   *W*

Soundness: 3   Surprise Value: 3

Caro-Kann: 3 ♕f3 dxe4

1 e4 c6 2 ♘c3 d5 3 ♕f3 dxe4 4 ♘xe4 *(38a)* is the critical line of the 3 ♕f3 system. The theoretical prescription for Black is to play ...♘d7 followed, after d2-d4, by ...♘df6 (i.e. *not* the normal knight in the main lines of the Caro) since this opens up an attack on the d4-pawn. White's choice then is essentially between safe but dull lines, in which he safeguards the d4-pawn, and more interesting, riskier lines in which he gambits it. We shall focus on the latter.

a) **4...♘f6 5 ♘xf6+** and now:

a1) **5...gxf6 6 ♗c4** is worse for Black than a standard Bronstein/Larsen since his queen's bishop has problems developing.

a2) **5...exf6 6 ♗c4 ♗d6** (6...♗c5? 7 ♗xf7+) 7 ♘e2 0-0 8 d4 ♘d7 9 0-0 ♘b6 10 ♗b3 a5 11 c4 a4 12 ♗c2 ± Short-Zilber, Hastings 1979.

b) **4...♘d7 5 d4** *(38b)* (5 ♕g3 ♘gf6 6 ♘xf6+ ♘xf6 7 ♗c4 ♗f5? 8 ♕b3 is a funny trap) and now:

b1) **5...♘gf6 6 ♗c4 e6** (6...♘b6 7 ♗d3 ♕xd4 8 ♘e2 gives White a certain amount of compensation for the pawn) 7 ♗g5 (7 ♘e2 ♘xe4 8 ♕xe4 ♘f6 9 ♕f3 ♗e7 10 ♗d2 0-0 11 0-0-0 ♗d7 12 h4 ± Hoffmann-Hastings, Philadelphia 1993) 7...♗e7 8 h4!? ♘xe4 9 ♕xe4 ♘f6 10 ♗xf6 ♗xf6 11 ♘f3 ♗d7 12 ♘e5 ♕e7 13 0-0-0 0-0-0 14 ♖h3 ♗xe5 15 dxe5 c5 16 ♖d6 ♗e8 17 ♖b3 +- ♖d7 18 ♗a6 ♖c7 19 ♗xb7+ ♖xb7 *(38c)* 20 ♖d8+! ♔xd8 21 ♖xb7 ♗d7 22 ♖xa7 ♕e8 23 ♕d3 f6 24 ♕d6 1-0 was a game Rossiter-Adams.

b2) **5...♘df6 6 ♗d3** *(38d)* (6 ♘xf6+
♗xf6 7 c3 ♗g4 8 ♕g3 e6 9 ♘f3 ♗xf3 10
♕xf3 ♕d5 11 ♕xd5 ♘xd5 12 ♗e2 is boring, but a shade better for White, Galego-
Danielsen, Debrecen Echt 1992; 6 c3 ♘xe4
7 ♕xe4 ♘f6 also leads to quieter play) and
now:

b21) **6...♗g4** 7 ♕f4 ♘xe4 8 ♕xg4 ♘gf6
9 ♕e2 ♕xd4 10 ♘f3 with at least some
compensation.

b22) **6...♘xe4** 7 ♕xe4 ♘f6 8 ♕h4 ♕a5+
(8...♕d5 9 ♘f3 ♗g4 10 c4 ♕e6+ 11 ♗e3
♗xf3 12 gxf3 g6 13 0-0-0 ♗g7 14 ♖hg1
0-0-0 15 ♖g5 with active play, Kichinski-
Mcdaniel, Livermore 1991) 9 ♗d2 ♕h5 10
♕xh5 ♘xh5 11 ♘f3 e6 12 c4 with a space
advantage, Schiller-Bowden, corr. 1991.

b23) **6...♕xd4** 7 ♘e2 and now:

b231) **7...♕d8** 8 ♗g5 ♗g4 (8...♘xe4 9
♗xe4 ♘f6 10 ♗xf6) 9 ♕g3 ♘xe4 (9...♗xe2
10 ♔xe2) 10 ♗xe4 ♗xe2 11 ♔xe2 ♘f6 12
♖hd1 ♕b6 13 ♗xf6 exf6 14 ♖d3 ♖d8 15
♖xd8+ ♕xd8 16 ♖d1 ♕c8 17 ♗f5 1-0
Sletebo-Wundhal, corr. 1982.

b232) **7...♕b6 8 ♗e3 ♕xb2 9 0-0 ♗g4**
(the alternatives are 9...♘xe4 10 ♗xe4 ♕f6
11 ♕g3, 9...♕a3 and 9...e5) **10 ♕g3** *(38e)*
and then:

b2321) **10...♘xe4** 11 ♕xg4 ♘gf6 (perhaps 11...♘d6!?) 12 ♕f3 ♘d6 (12...♕e5!?
13 ♖ab1) 13 ♖fb1 ♕a3 14 ♖xb7 ♘xb7 15
♕xc6+ ♘d7 16 ♗b5 ♖d8 17 ♕xb7 and
Black won't get out alive.

b2322) **10...♗xe2** 11 ♖ab1 ♘xe4 (maybe
11...♕xa2!?) 12 ♕c7 ♕c3 13 ♕xb7 ♖d8 14
♗xe4 f5 *(38f)* 15 ♗xc6+ ♔f7 16 ♕c7 ♕f6
17 ♕xd8 ♕xc6 and Black has problems
completing his development.

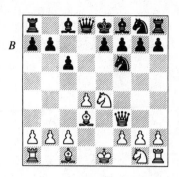

38d: after 6 ♗d3

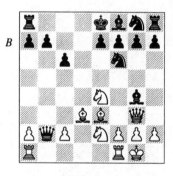

38e: after 10 ♕g3

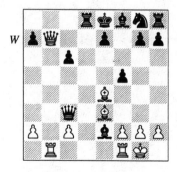

38f: after 14...f5

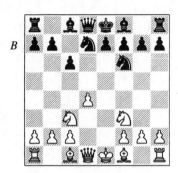

39a: after 6 ②c3

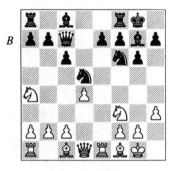

39b: after 12 ②f1

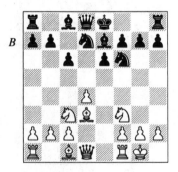

39c: after 8 0-0

Surprise 39   **W**

Soundness: 3   Surprise Value: 2

Caro-Kann 5 ②f3 and 6 ②c3

The variation **1 e4 c6 2 d4 d5 3 ②c3 dxe4 4 ②xe4 ②d7** is looking very sound for Black nowadays. Since the modern main lines are making so little impression on it, I suggest dredging **5 ②f3 ②gf6 6 ②c3** *(39a)* out of the archives. It has been played by Smyslov, Spassky, Bronstein and Tal (the latter two winning brilliancies in the line), so can't be too bad! Here are some variations:

a) **6...豐c7** 7 ②d3 e6 8 0-0 ②d6 9 罩e1 0-0 10 豐e2 ②f4 11 ②e4 ②xc1 12 罩axc1 b5 13 ②e5 ②b7 14 ②xd7 ②xd7 15 豐h5 is good for White, Smyslov-Fuster, Budapest 1949.

b) **6...②b6** (possibly Black's best reply) 7 ②f4 ②f5 8 ②d3 ②xd3 9 豐xd3 e6 10 0-0 ②e7 11 罩fe1 0-0 (Antoshin-Flohr, Moscow 1955) and now White ought to try the natural 12 罩ad1 ②bd5 13 ②e5.

c) **6...g6** 7 ②e2 ②g7 8 0-0 0-0 9 罩e1 (White avoids putting his bishops on squares where they can be hit by the black knights) 9...②b6 10 h3 ②bd5 11 ②a4 豐c7 12 ②f1 *(39b)* 12...罩d8 13 c4 ②b6 14 ②c3 ②e6 15 b3 and there has arisen a position similar to those arising from the Kengis Variation of the Alekhine – this is not a good one, as counterplay is lacking. Black got squashed in Popović-Spiridonov, Bajmok 1980.

d) **6...e6 7 ②d3** and then:

d1) **7...②d6** 8 0-0 豐c7 (8...0-0 9 罩e1 豐c7 10 豐e2 a6 11 ②e4 ②xe4 12 豐xe4 ②f6 13 豐h4 ②e7 14 ②g5 with a winning attack, Hoen-Sande, Norwegian Ch (Oslo) 1975) 9 豐e2 0-0 10 ②e4 ②f4 11 c4 b6 12 b3 ②xc1 13 罩axc1 ± Pilnik-O'Kelly, Bled 1950.

d2) **7...♗e7 8 0-0** *(39c)* and here:

d21) **8...0-0** 9 ♗f4 c5 10 ♘b5 (10 ♖e1 b6 11 ♕e2 cxd4 12 ♘xd4 ♗b7 13 ♘xe6 fxe6 14 ♕xe6+ ♖f7 15 ♗c4 1-0 Kitces-Wygle, telephone 1982) 10...♘d5 11 ♗g3 a6 12 c4 axb5 13 cxd5 exd5 14 ♕c2 ± Pilnik-Luckis, Mar del Plata 1950.

d22) **8...c5** 9 ♕e2 *(39d)* 9...cxd4 (9...0-0 10 ♖d1 cxd4 11 ♘xd4 ♖e8 12 ♗c4 a6 13 ♗g5 ♕a5 14 ♗h4 ♘f8 15 ♘b3 ♕b6 16 a4 ♘g6 17 ♗g3 e5 18 a5 ♕c7 19 ♘d5 ♘xd5 20 ♗xd5 ♗f8 21 ♖a4 ± Gligorić-Rossolimo, Cheltenham 1951) 10 ♘xd4 0-0 11 ♗g5 ♘c5 12 ♖ad1 ♘xd3 13 ♖xd3 ♕c7 14 ♘db5 ♕c6 15 ♖fd1 b6 16 ♘d4 ♕c7 17 ♖g3 ♔h8 18 ♘cb5 ♕b7 19 ♕e5 a6 20 ♘c3 ♘d7 *(39e)* 21 ♗h6 1-0 Bronstein-Kotov, Moscow Ch 1946.

d3) **7...c5** 8 ♕e2 cxd4 (8...♗e7 9 ♗f4 a6 10 0-0-0 ♕a5 11 d5 with a massive advantage, Ghizdavu-Rotariu, Romanian Ch (Bucharest) 1973) 9 ♘xd4 ♗c5 (9...♘c5 10 ♗b5+ keeps annoying pressure on Black) 10 ♘b3 ♗d6 11 ♗g5 a6 12 0-0-0 ♕c7 13 ♔b1 0-0 14 ♘e4 ♗e5 15 f4 ♗xf4 16 ♘xf6+ ♘xf6 17 ♗xf6 gxf6 18 ♕g4+ ♔h8 19 ♖hf1 ♗e5 *(39f)* 20 ♗xh7 f5 21 ♕h4 ♔g7 22 ♖f3 ♖e8 23 g4 f4 24 g5 ♔f8 25 ♖xf4 ♗xf4 26 ♕h6+ ♔e7 27 ♕f6+ ♔f8 28 g6 ♗h6 29 ♖f1 1-0 Tal-Shamkovich, USSR Ch (Baku) 1972.

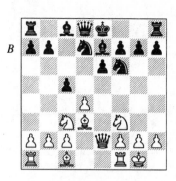

39d: after 9 ♕e2

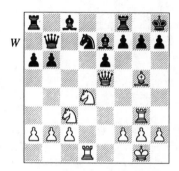

39e: after 20...♘d7

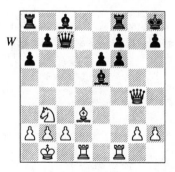

39f: after 19...♗e5

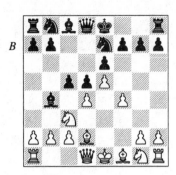

40a: after 6 f4

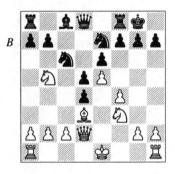

40b: after 10 ♗d3

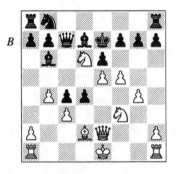

40c: after 16 f5

Surprise 40   W

Soundness: 3   Surprise Value: 3

French Winawer: Icelandic

After **1 e4 e6 2 d4 d5 3 ♘c3 ♗b4 4 e5 c5**, the line **5 ♗d2 ♘e7 6 f4!?** *(40a)* is a speciality of Icelandic GM Thorhallsson. White seems to get dangerous play however Black responds:

a) **6...cxd4** 7 ♘b5 ♗xd2+ 8 ♕xd2 0-0 9 ♘f3 ♘bc6 10 ♗d3 *(40b)* 10...f6 11 exf6 ♖xf6 12 0-0-0 ♗d7 13 ♘bxd4 ♕b6 14 ♖he1 h6 15 ♔b1 ♘xd4 16 ♘xd4 ♘c6 17 ♘f3 ♗e8 18 ♘e5 ♘xe5 19 ♖xe5 with a clear plus for White, Thorhallsson-Blees, Hafnarfjordur 1995.

b) **6...0-0** 7 ♘f3 f6 8 ♗d3 ♘bc6 9 a3 ♗xc3 10 bxc3 fxe5 11 ♗xh7+!? ♔xh7 12 ♘g5+ ♔g8 13 ♕h5 and White's attack is enough for a draw at least, Thorhallsson-Kinsman, Hafnarfjordur 1997.

c) **6...♘bc6** 7 dxc5 ♘f5 8 ♘f3 ♗xc5 9 ♗d3 ♘h4 10 ♘xh4 ♕xh4+ 11 g3! ♕d8 (11...♕h3 12 ♗f1) 12 a3 f5?! (12...a6 13 ♕g4) 13 exf6 ♕xf6 14 ♕e2 0-0 15 0-0-0 gave White the advantage in W.Watson-Harley, British Ch 1994.

d) **6...♘f5** 7 ♘f3 cxd4 8 ♘b5 ♗c5 9 b4 ♗b6?! 10 ♗d3 ♗d7 11 g4 ♘e3 12 ♘d6+ ♔e7 13 ♕e2 ♕c7 14 c3! ♘c4 15 ♗xc4 dxc4 16 f5 *(40c)* (White has a strong attack) 16...♗c6 (16...exf5 17 gxf5; 16...d3 17 f6+ ♔f8 18 fxg7+ ♔xg7 19 ♖h6+; 16...♘c6 17 f6+ gxf6 18 exf6+ ♔xf6 19 ♗f4; 16...h6!? 17 f6+) and now, in Thorhallsson-Djurhuus, Gausdal Eikrem mem 1996, White should have played 17 fxe6 fxe6 18 ♖f1 d3 (18...♖f8 19 ♘xd4) 19 ♘d4 winning – analysis by Djurhuus.

Surprise 41 W

Soundness: 4 Surprise Value: 2

Winawer: Paoli Variation

In the French Poisoned Pawn, **1 e4 e6 2 d4 d5 3 ♘c3 ♗b4 4 e5 c5 5 a3 ♗xc3+ 6 bxc3 ♘e7 7 ♕g4 cxd4 8 ♕xg7 ♖g8 9 ♕xh7 ♕c7**, the move **10 ♔d1** *(41a)*, although far from new, still causes surprise. It was introduced in 1957 by the Italian, Dr Enrico Paoli, with the idea of meeting **10...♘bc6** (or 10...♘d7; 10...♕xe5 11 ♘f3 ♕f6 12 cxd4 is good for White) with **11 ♘f3!? ♘xe5** (11...dxc3 is seen in the next Surprise) **12 ♗f4! ♕xc3 13 ♘xe5 ♕xa1+ 14 ♗c1**:

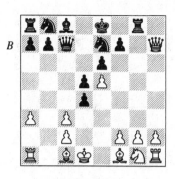

41a: after 10 ♔d1

a) **14...d3?! 15 ♕xf7+ ♔d8 16 ♕f6!** (threatening to win Black's queen) **16...dxc2+ 17 ♔d2 ♕d4+ 18 ♗d3** and then:

a1) **18...♔e8?** 19 ♗e2 ♗d7 20 ♗e3 ♕b2 21 ♖c1 ♖c8 22 ♘xd7 d4 *(41b)* (Bronstein-Uhlmann, Zagreb 1965) 23 ♘b8!! wins.

a2) **18...♕c5** 19 ♔e2 ♗d7 20 ♗e3 d4 (20...♕xa3) 21 ♗xd4! c1♕?! (21...♕d5) 22 ♖xc1 ♕xc1 23 ♘f7+ ♔e8 (23...♔c7 24 ♕xe7) 24 ♘d6+ ♔d8 (B.Stein-Beliavsky, London Lloyds Bank 1985) 25 ♘xb7+ ♔c7 (25...♔e8 26 ♗c5 wins; 25...♔c8 26 ♕xe7) 26 ♕xe7 ♕c6 27 ♘c5 *(41c)* and Black is overpowered, e.g. 27...a6 28 ♗e4 ♖ae8 (28...♕b5+ 29 ♔e3) 29 ♕f6 ♕b5+ 30 ♗d3. This game is a good example of the surprise effect of 10 ♔d1. Beliavsky, then amongst the absolute world elite, had just taken up the French, and had carefully prepared the lines he was likely to face. The footnote on 10 ♔d1, however, was not subjected to the normal scrutiny.

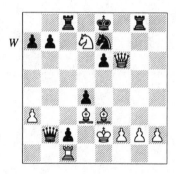

41b: after 22...d4

b) **14...♖f8 15 ♗d3 ♗d7** (the continuation 15...♘c6 16 ♘xf7! ♖xf7 17 ♕g8+ ♔e7

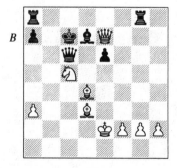

42c: after 27 ♘c5

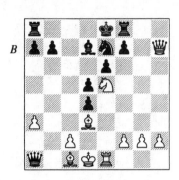

41d: after 16 ♖e1

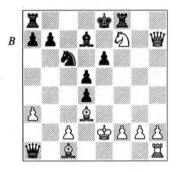

41e: after 17 ♘xf7

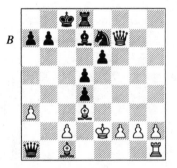

41f: after 18 ♕xf7

18 ♔e2 works well for White) and now White has a choice:

b1) **16 ♖e1** *(41d)* is very interesting:

b11) **16...♘c6** 17 ♘xf7 ♖xf7 18 ♗g6 0-0-0 19 ♕xf7 e5 20 ♔e2 e4 21 ♔f1 ♕c3 22 ♗g5 ♘e5 (22...♘e7, Schmid-Pachman, 1967, 23 ♗h5! wins) 23 ♕xd5 ♘f3 24 ♖b1 ♕c7 25 ♗xd8 ♘d2+ 26 ♔e1 1-0 Fuchs-Uhlmann, 1966.

b12) **16...♗a4** 17 ♔e2 ♕c3 18 ♗h6 ♗xc2 19 ♗xf8 ♗xd3+ 20 ♘xd3 ♘g6? 21 ♗b4 ♕c2+ 22 ♔f1 ♕xd3+ 23 ♔g1 0-0-0 24 ♕xf7 ♔b8 25 ♖c1 ♔a8 26 ♕c7 1-0 Ankerst-Nikolić, Yugoslavia 1965.

b2) **16 ♔e2** gives Black a choice:

b21) **16...♘c6?** 17 ♘xf7! *(41e)* 17...♖xf7 18 ♕g8+ ♖f8 19 ♗g6+ ♔e7 20 ♕g7+ ♔d6 21 ♗f4+ with a large advantage for White, Matulović-Camilleri, 1967.

b22) **16...a6** 17 ♗h6 ♕xh1 18 ♗xf8 0-0-0 19 ♗xe7 ♖e8 20 ♕xf7 ♗a4 21 ♗d6 1-0 Jovcić-Savić, corr.

b23) **16...f6** 17 ♗h6 ♕xa3 was apparently played in a game Tal-Bronstein, Moscow training match (4) 1966, leading to a win for White, but I'm suspicious of the accuracy of the data.

b24) **16...0-0-0** 17 ♘xf7 ♖xf7 18 ♕xf7 *(41f)* 18...♘c6 (18...♖e8 19 ♖e1 e5 20 ♔f1 e4 21 ♗e2 ♕c3 22 ♗g5 ♕xa3, Matulović-Jahr, Reggio Emilia 1967/8, 23 ♖d1 "and Black has not solved his opening problems" – A.Martin and B.Stein) 19 ♖e1 ♘e5 20 ♕e7 ♕a2 (20...♘xd3? 21 ♕xd8+ ♔xd8 22 ♗g5+) 21 ♔f1 ♖e8 22 ♕d6 ♘c4 23 ♕c5+ ♔b8 24 ♕xd4 e5 25 ♗xc4! ♕xc4+ 26 ♕xc4 dxc4 27 ♗b2 with a winning ending for White, Taruffi-Fricker, La Spezia 1974.

Surprise 42   W

Soundness: 4   Surprise Value: 2

Winawer: Paoli, 11...dxc3

42a: after 11...dxc3

The main line after **1 e4 e6 2 d4 d5 3 ♘c3 ♗b4 4 e5 c5 5 a3 ♗xc3+ 6 bxc3 ♘e7 7 ♕g4 cxd4 8 ♕xg7 ♖g8 9 ♕xh7 ♕c7 10 ♔d1** is considered to be **10...♘bc6 11 ♘f3 dxc3** *(42a)*. Here are some ideas for White:

a) **12 ♘g5** is the main line, but not necessarily best:

a1) **12...♖f8** 13 f4 ♗d7 14 ♗d3 (14 ♕d3 0-0-0 15 ♕xc3 ♔b8, Minić-Korchnoi, Bucharest 1966, 16 a4 ± Ivkov) 14...♕b6 15 ♖e1 0-0-0 16 ♘xf7 ♖xf7 17 ♕xf7 ± O'Kelly-Pietzsch, Havana Capablanca mem 1965.

a2) **12...♘xe5 13 f4** *(42b)* and then:

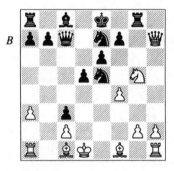

42b: after 13 f4

a21) **13...f6** 14 fxe5 fxg5 15 ♕h5+ ♔d8 16 ♗xg5 ♕c5 (Popović-J.Watson, New York 1981) 17 ♗d3!? with ♖f1 to follow.

a22) **13...♖xg5** 14 fxg5 ♘5g6 and now 15 h4!? is sharp and very interesting.

a3) **12...♕xe5** 13 ♕xf7+ ♔d7 is unclear – Korchnoi. This awaits a practical test.

b) **12 ♖b1!?** ♗d7 13 ♗g5 0-0-0 14 ♕d3 ♖xg5 15 ♘xg5 ♘xe5 16 ♕d4 ♔b8 17 ♗a6 b6 18 ♖b3 f6 (Minić-Ivkov, Titograd 1965) and now 19 ♘h7 looks interesting, and not at all bad.

c) **12 ♗f4** ♕b6 and the black queen demonstrates its nuisance value.

d) **12 h4!?** ♕b6 13 ♗e3 (White spends a move to block off the queen's action against f2) 13...d4 14 ♗g5 ♗d7 15 ♗d3 0-0-0 16 ♔e2 ♕c5 17 ♖hb1 a6 18 ♕e4 ♖de8 19 g3 *(42c)* with a messy position, where White enjoys the better prospects, Mestel-Short, Hastings 1983.

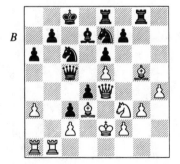

42c: after 19 g3

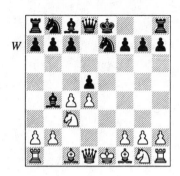

43a: after 5...♘e7

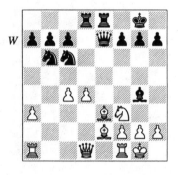

43b: after 15...♖ad8

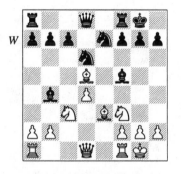

43c: after 13...♘e7

Surprise 43   B

Soundness: 4   Surprise Value: 2

French Exchange with 4 c4

Here we examine an idea for Black in the line **1 e4 e6 2 d4 d5 3 exd5 exd5 4 c4**, which had been proving quite annoying for Black. Tal Shaked and Thomas Luther have shown that **4...♗b4+ 5 ♘c3 ♘e7** *(43a)* gives interesting possibilities. Note that it is important that the knight goes to e7, via where it can bring more immediate pressure to bear on the d4-pawn than it could from f6. After **6 ♘f3** (6 a3 ♗xc3+ 7 bxc3 0-0 8 ♘f3 is line 'a') **6...0-0** there is:

a) **7 a3** (White probably cannot afford this) **7...♗xc3+ 8 bxc3 ♘bc6** and then:

a1) **9 c5 b6 10 ♗e2 bxc5 11 dxc5 a5 12 0-0 ♗a6** and Black's structural superiority prevailed in Mallahi-Shaked, Cala Galdana U-18 Wch 1996.

a2) **9 ♗e2 dxc4 10 ♗xc4 ♘d5 11 ♗d2 ♖e8+ 12 ♗e2 ♕e7 13 c4 ♘b6 14 ♗e3 ♗g4 15 0-0 ♖ad8** *(43b)* (White's centre is crumbling) **16 d5 ♗xf3 17 gxf3 ♘e5 18 ♕b3 ♘bxc4! 19 ♗xc4 ♘xf3+ 20 ♔g2 ♕e4** wins on the spot, Santo-Roman – Shaked, Cannes 1997.

b) **7 ♗e2 dxc4 8 ♗xc4 ♗g4 9 0-0 ♘bc6 10 ♗e3 ♘f5 11 ♕d3 ♘d6 12 ♗d5** (12 ♘e5 ♗f5 13 ♕e2 ♗xc3 14 ♘xc6 bxc6 15 bxc3 ♘xc4 16 ♕xc4 ♕d5 brings about drawish simplifications, T.Reich-M.Schäfer, Bundesliga 1994) **12...♗f5 13 ♕d1 ♘e7!** *(43c)* **14 ♗b3 c6 15 ♘e5 ♔h8 16 ♖c1 f6 17 ♘d3 ♗xc3 18 bxc3 ♘d5 19 ♘f4 ♘xe3 20 fxe3** with good play against the weak e3-pawn, Waitzkin-Shaked, Bermuda 1997.

Surprise 44 *B*

Soundness: 4   Surprise Value: 2

Winckelman-Reimer Gambit

Here I present a good reply to this dangerous gambit against the Winawer French: **1 e4 e6 2 d4 d5 3 ♘c3 ♗b4 4 a3 ♗xc3+ 5 bxc3 dxe4 6 f3**. This is a bit like a Blackmar-Diemer Gambit, but more justified by the disappearance of Black's important defensive king's bishop. Now **6...e5** *(44a)* is Hübner's recommendation.

a) **7 fxe4 ♕h4+ 0-1** De Smet-Hoffmann, corr 1991. One can but hope!

b) **7 ♗c4** can be answered in a number of ways; 7...♘c6 looks sensible.

c) **7 ♕e2 exd4 8 ♕xe4+ ♕e7 9 cxd4 ♗f5 10 ♕xe7+ ♘xe7 11 c3 0-0 12 ♗c4 ♘d7 13 ♗f4 ♘b6 14 ♗b3 ♘ed5 15 ♗d2 ♖fe8+ 16 ♔f2 ♗d3** is a bit better for Black, Oller-Reichert, theme corr 1993.

d) **7 a4** is a logical move, freeing a3 for the bishop. One danger for Black is that his lack of dark-square control will give White attacking chances. However, 7...exd4 (7...♘f6 8 ♗a3) 8 cxd4 c5 *(44b)* blocks off the diagonal. After 9 ♗b5+, rather than **9...♘c6 10 d5 a6 11 ♗xc6+ bxc6 12 dxc6 ♕xd1+ 13 ♔xd1 exf3 14 ♘xf3 ♗g4 15 ♖e1+** with good play for White, Tripolsky-Kvitko, Dnepropetrovsk 1993, I suggest **9...♗d7 10 dxc5 ♘f6**.

e) **7 ♗e3 exd4! 8 cxd4 ♘h6!** *(44c)* (threatening ...♘f5 and maintaining the possibility of ...♕h4+) 9 fxe4 ♕h4+ 10 ♔d2 ♕xe4 11 ♘f3 ♘f5 12 ♗b5+ ♘c6 13 ♖e1 0-0 14 c3 ♘xe3 15 ♖xe3 ♕f4 16 ♕f1 ♘a5 17 ♖b1 ♗e6 with simply an extra pawn, Grabarczyk-Gdanski, Polish Cht (Lubniewice) 1993.

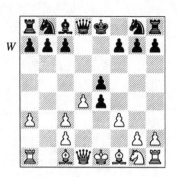

44a: after 6...e5

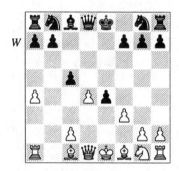

44b: after 8...c5

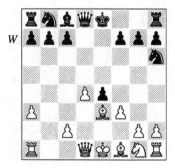

44c: after 8...♘h6

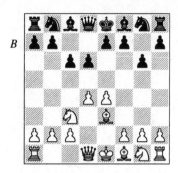

45a: after 4 ♗e3

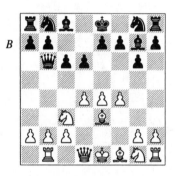

45b: after 6 ♖b1

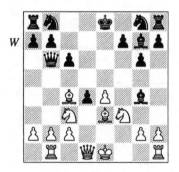

45c: after 9...exd4

Surprise 45   W

Soundness: 4   Surprise Value: 2

Accelerated Gurgenidze

This is a tip for those who want to play the Austrian Attack against the Pirc/Modern, while dodging the Accelerated Gurgenidze, which is a little move-order trick devised by Dave Norwood: **1 e4 g6 2 d4 d6 3 ♘c3 c6.** The idea is that Black meets 4 f4 with 4...d5 5 e5, seeming to lose a tempo (...d7-d6-d5, rather than ...♗f8-g7 and ...d7-d5 as in the normal Gurgenidze), but in fact gaining one, since the bishop is better on f8 than g7 in this structure (thus ...d7-d6-d5 is a tempo faster than ...d7-d5 and ...♗f8-g7-f8)!

However, we play **4 ♗e3** *(45a)*. Then 4...d5 makes no sense (a move down on a type of Gurgenidze – without f4 – that Black was seeking to avoid), while **4...♗g7 5 f4** reaches an Austrian Attack, as desired.

This is not an easy type of Austrian Attack for Black. The move ...c6 only really makes sense if a counterattack with ...♕b6 is viable. However, this does not appear to be the case here. A critical line runs **5...♕b6 6 ♖b1** *(45b)*:

a) **6...f5 7 e5!** dxe5 8 fxe5 ♗xe5 9 ♘f3 ♗g7 10 ♗c4 gives White very good compensation for the pawn, C.Hansen-Todorčević, Rome 1988.

b) **6...♘h6 7 ♘f3 f5** (highly artificial) 8 e5 ♘f7 9 ♕d2 ♕c7 10 ♗d3 with a definite plus for White, C.Hansen-Lau, Palma de Mallorca 1989.

c) **6...e5 7 ♘f3 ♗g4 8** fxe5 dxe5 9 ♗c4! exd4 *(45c)* 10 ♗xf7+! ♔f8 11 ♗f2 and Black's king is insecure.

Surprise 46 B

Soundness: 2   Surprise Value: 4

Modern: 3...d5

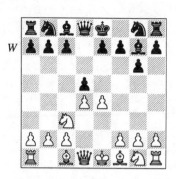

46a: after 3...d5

After **1 e4 g6 2 d4 ♗g7 3 ♘c3**, one of the most startling moves at Black's disposal is **3...d5** *(46a)*. Despite its odd appearance, it seems White can only keep a modest advantage. After **4 exd5 ♘f6**, if White just lets Black recapture, then he will be very comfortable since, with the knight on c3, White cannot play c2-c4, and must deal with the possibility of ...♘xc3. Thus:

a) **5 ♗b5+ ♘bd7 6 ♘f3** (6 ♘ge2!?) 6...0-0 7 0-0 ♘b6 8 ♖e1 ♘bxd5 9 ♘xd5 ♘xd5 10 h3 with just an edge for White, Lederman-Vydeslaver, Beersheba 1991.

b) **5 ♗c4** and then:

b1) **5...0-0** 6 ♗g5 (6 ♘ge2 ♘bd7 7 ♗b3 ♘b6 8 ♘f4 a5 9 a4 ♗f5 10 0-0 ± Yudasin-Vydeslaver, Beersheba 1992) 6...c6 7 ♗xf6 ♗xf6 8 ♘ge2 ♗g7 9 ♗b3 b6 10 ♕d2 ♗b7 11 dxc6 ♘xc6 12 ♖d1 ♕d7 13 0-0 ♖ad8 14 d5 ♘a5 15 ♕f4 ♘xb3 16 axb3 ♕c8 17 ♖d2 ♖d6 18 ♖fd1 ♖fd8 19 ♕e3 ♖8d7 *(46b)* 20 ♘f4 ♗h6 21 ♘ce2 g5 22 ♘h3 ♖xd5 led to a draw in Tal-Palacios, Seville 1989.

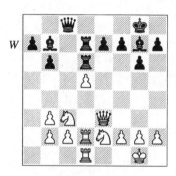

46b: after 19...♖8d7

b2) **5...♘bd7 6 ♗g5!** *(46c)* and now:

b21) **6...♘b6** 7 ♗xf6 ♗xf6 8 ♗b3 a5 (8...c6 9 dxc6 ♕xd4 10 ♕xd4 ♗xd4 11 ♘ge2 ♗xc3+ 12 ♘xc3 bxc6 13 0-0-0 ± Aseev-K.Schulz, German Cup 1991) 9 a4 0-0 10 ♘ge2 c6 11 dxc6 bxc6 12 0-0 ♗a6 with some compensation, Keitlinghaus-Vokač, Prague 1992.

b22) **6...0-0** 7 ♗b3 ♘b6 8 ♕f3 ♗d7 9 ♕f4 (Sadler-Turner, British Ch (Hove) 1997) 9...a5 10 a4 ♗f5 looks OK for Black.

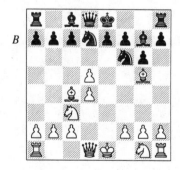

46c: after 6 ♗g5

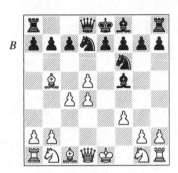

47a: after 6 c4

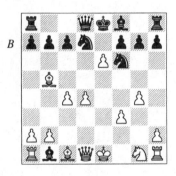

47b: after 8 dxe6

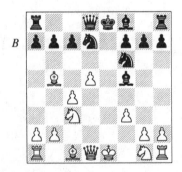

47c: after 9 ♘c3

Surprise 47   *W*

Soundness: 3   Surprise Value: 3

Portuguese Gambit: 5 ♗b5+

The gambit **1 e4 d5 2 exd5 ♘f6 3 d4 ♗g4** has been terrifying 1 e4 players for a few years now. There have been plenty of games where Black's development advantage has become overwhelming, and White has lost a horrible miniature. Many recent games have seen White chickening out completely, with 4 ♘f3 or 4 ♗e2.

Here I advocate **4 f3 ♗f5 5 ♗b5+** (not 5 c4 e6 6 dxe6 ♘c6!) **5...♘bd7 6 c4** *(47a)*.

Now **6...e6** (6...a6 is seen in the next Surprise) gives White two options:

a) **7 g4!??** ♗xb1 (7...♘xg4 8 ♗xd7+ ♔xd7 9 fxg4 ♕h4+ 10 ♔f1 ♗xg4 11 ♘f3 ♕h3+ 12 ♔f2 +− Søbjerg-Schmied, Copenhagen 1995) 8 dxe6! *(47b)* 8...fxe6 9 ♖xb1 c6 10 ♗a4 ♗b4+ 11 ♗d2 ♘xg4?! (11...♕a5 is critical) 12 ♗xb4 ♕h4+ 13 ♔e2 ♕f2+ 14 ♔d3 +− Rodriguez Uria-Ribeiro, Candas 1992.

b) **7 dxe6 ♗xe6 8 d5 ♗f5 9 ♘c3** *(47c)* and now:

b1) **9...♗c5** 10 ♕e2+ ♕e7 11 g4 ♗d3 12 ♕xe7+ ♗xe7 13 ♗f4 0-0-0 14 0-0-0 ♗g6 (Renet-Galego, Eupen 1994) 15 ♗xd7+! ♖xd7 16 h4 h5 17 g5 ♘h7 18 ♘ge2 ±.

b2) **9...♗b4** 10 ♘ge2 0-0 11 ♗xd7! ♘xd7 12 0-0 ♘c5 (after 12...♘e5, Emms mentions the greedy 13 b3 and 13 ♔h1 ♘xc4 14 ♕d4 ±) 13 ♘f4!? ♖e8 14 ♘ce2 ♕f6 15 ♘g3 ♘d7 16 ♔h1 (16 ♘xf5 is possible too) 16...♗d6 17 ♘gh5 ♕e5 18 g4 ♗g6 19 ♘g3 ♘c5 20 ♘xg6 hxg6 21 f4 ♕e7 22 ♔g2 with a sound extra pawn, Agnos-C.Santos, Pula Echt 1997.

Surprise 48   W

Soundness: 3   Surprise Value: 3

Portuguese: 5 &b5+, 6...a6

After **1 e4 d5 2 exd5 &f6 3 d4 &g4 4 f3
&f5 5 &b5+ &bd7 6 c4**, there is the sharp
6...a6. The point is that after **7 &a4**, Black
has **7...b5!? 8 cxb5 &b6! 9 bxa6+ &xa4 10
&xa4+ &d7**, smashing open the position and
gaining plenty of counterplay. Instead White
should play **7 &xd7+ &xd7 8 &e2** *(48a)*.

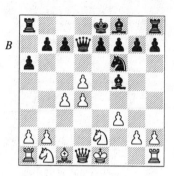

48a: after 8 &e2

a) **8...b5 9 b3 bxc4 10 bxc4 e6 11 dxe6
&xe6 12 &a4+ &d7 13 &f2! &d6 14 c5
&xb1 15 &xb1 &e7 16 &e3 g5 17 d5!** +–
C.Cobb-Hebden, British League (4NCL)
1997/8.

b) **8...0-0-0 9 0-0 e6 10 &bc3 exd5 11 c5**
returns the pawn for a big attack, Kokkila-
Aijälä, Jyväskylä 1996.

c) **8...e6 9 dxe6 &xe6 10 b3 0-0-0 11 0-0
&c5 12 &h1 &xd4 13 &xd4 &d7 14 &b2
c5 15 b4 cxd4 16 b5** *(48b)* and now:

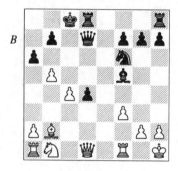

48b: after 16 b5

c1) **16...&he8 17 bxa6 bxa6 18 &a3 d3
19 c5 &e2 20 &xf6 gxf6 21 &c4 &c7 22
&d6 &h3** *(48c)* **23 &g1 &b8 24 &b1 &f5 25
&xb8 &xb8 26 &b3+ &a8 27 &b1 1-0**
G.Ruben-Mongin, IECG 1996.

c2) **16...axb5 17 &a3 bxc4 18 &xc4 &b8
19 &a3 &d5** (19...&e6!? **20 &c1 &a6 21
&c5 &e6**, Palac-Liardet, Cannes 1997, and
now White should play **22 &b2**, planning to
eliminate the d-pawn before targeting the
black king again) **20 &c1 &he8 21 &d2 &e6
22 &a5 &b5** (22...&d7 **23 &c4 &a6 24 &b4
&xa5 25 &xa5 &xc4 26 &c1** ± Slipak-del
Castillo, Buenos Aires 1992) **23 &c5 &a8
24 a4 &a6 25 &b3 &d3 26 &g1 &e2 27
&b4 &h5 28 &b6 &de8 29 &c5 &e5 30
&gd1 1-0** Lanka-Hauchard, Torcy 1991.

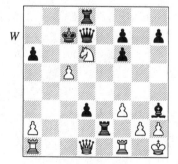

48c: after 22...&h3

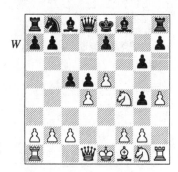

49a: after 9...c5

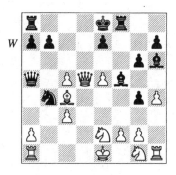

49b: after 15...♘xb4

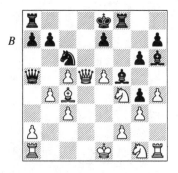

49c: after 15 b4

Surprise 49   *B*

Soundness: 3   Surprise Value: 3

Alekhine: 2 ♘c3 with 4...f6

After **1 e4 ♘f6 2 ♘c3 d5 3 e5 ♘e4 4 ♘ce2**, the move **4...f6** (rather than the standard 4...d4) has been viewed with suspicion for many years in view of the forceful line **5 d3 ♘g5 6 ♗xg5 fxg5 7 h4**. Black must reply **7...g4**, when **8 ♘f4** (8 d4 c5 9 dxc5 ♘c6 is likely to reach the same position after 10 ♘f4 g6) **8...g6 9 d4 c5!?** *(49a)* (my novelty from some years ago, but until I did some new analysis for this book I didn't trust it) seems viable for Black. **10 dxc5 ♘c6** (10...d4 11 ♗b5+ ♘c6 is probably asking a bit too much of the position) **11 ♕xd5 ♕a5+** (11...♗f5 was played in Feistenauer-Petschar, Austrian Cht 1996, but White's response, 12 ♕xd8+ ♖xd8 13 ♗d3 ♗h6 14 ♗xf5 gxf5 15 ♘ge2 ♘xe5 16 ♖d1 =, was feeble) **12 c3 ♗h6** and now:

a) **13 ♗c4 ♖f8 14 ♘fe2** (14 ♘ge2 ♗xf4 15 ♘xf4 ♖xf4 16 ♕g8+ ♔d7; for 14 g3 see line 'b') 14...♗f5 15 b4 (15 ♘d4 ♘xd4 leads to nothing good for White after 16 ♕xd4 ♖d8 or 16 ♕xb7 ♖d8) 15...♘xb4 *(49b)* 16 ♕xb7 (16 cxb4 ♕xb4+ 17 ♔f1 ♖d8) 16...♘c2+ 17 ♔f1 ♘e3+ 18 ♔e1 ♘c2+ 19 ♔f1 repeating.

b) **13 g3 ♗f5 14 ♗c4 ♖f8 15 b4** *(49c)* 15...♕c7?! (15...♘xb4 16 ♕xb7 ♘c2+ is not too convincing either, but 15...♕a3!? is absolutely OK for Black) 16 ♘ge2 ♖d8 17 ♘e6 ♗xe6 18 ♕xe6 ♗d2+ 19 ♔f1 ♕xe5 20 ♖d1 (20 ♕xe5 ♘xe5 21 ♗b5+) 20...♗xc3 (20...♕xe6 21 ♗xe6 ♗e3 22 ♖xd8+ ♘xd8 ±) 21 ♖xd8+ ♔xd8 22 b5 ♕xe6 23 ♗xe6 ♘d4 24 ♗xg4 ± C.Baker-Burgess, Bristol tt 1991.

Surprise 50   *W*

Soundness: 2   Surprise Value: 5

Alekhine: 3 ♘a3?!!

A considerable psychological benefit can be achieved by playing a move that looks ridiculous, yet is viable. Such an effect can be achieved after **1 e4 ♘f6 2 e5 ♘d5** with the move **3 ♘a3** *(50a)*. This idea was suggested to me by my young clubmate Simon Buckley. While I don't think it's much of a try for advantage, I can't find a way for Black to take advantage of White's strange move, and it is possible to land in trouble by trying too hard to do so. The idea is to play the knight to c4 to give the e5-pawn support without needing to push the d-pawn just yet, and it can journey onward to e3 if kicked.

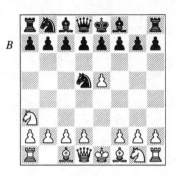

50a: after 3 ♘a3

Some variations:

a) **3...♘c6** will be answered by 4 ♘f3.

b) **3...e6** encourages 4 ♘c4.

c) **3...d6** 4 ♘c4 and then:

c1) **4...b5** 5 ♘e3 (the attack on b5 saves White's pawn) 5...♘xe3 (5...dxe5 6 ♗xb5+ c6 leaves White structurally better) 6 dxe3 (or 6 fxe3) 6...a6 *(50b)* is an odd type of position – I think I prefer White.

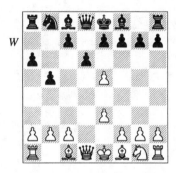

50b: after 6...a6

c2) **4...♗f5!?** 5 d4 ♘c6 (5...♘b4?! 6 ♘e3; 5...♘d7) 6 ♘f3 ♘cb4 7 ♘a3 and I don't see where Black is going.

c3) **4...dxe5** 5 ♘xe5 ♘d7 (5...♕d6; 5...♗f5?! 6 ♕f3) 6 ♘gf3 ♘xe5 7 ♘xe5 should be compared with the 'mainstream' line 3 d4 d6 4 ♘f3 dxe5 5 ♘xe5 g6 6 ♘d2 ♗g7 7 ♘df3.

c4) **4...♘c6** 5 ♘f3 ♗g4 6 exd6 exd6 7 ♗e2 ♘f4 8 ♘e3 *(50c)* 8...♘xe2 9 ♘xg4 ♘xc1 10 ♖xc1 has forced some simplifications, but White's knights are active.

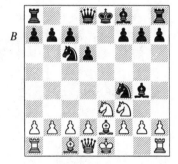

50c: after 8 ♘e3

51a: after 4...e5

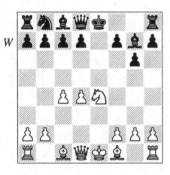

51b: after 7...♗g7

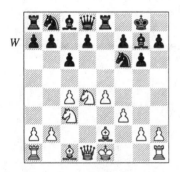

51c: after 8...c6

Surprise 51   *B*

Soundness: 4   Surprise Value: 4

Anti-Anti-Grünfeld

1 ♘f3 ♘f6 2 c4 g6 3 ♘c3 ♗g7 4 e4 is a move-order used quite often by those as White who are willing to play a Réti, English or King's Indian (after 4...d6), but wish to stop Black playing the Grünfeld. Then **4...e5!?** *(51a)* will come as quite a surprise. This is related to the Adorjan line 1 c4 g6 2 e4 e5, into which it can transpose. 4...e5 was first played by Marshall in 1941, in one of the very few examples I have found prior to Rowson's use of it in 1997. The critical line runs **5 ♘xe5 ♘xe4 6 ♘xe4** (not 6 ♘xf7?? ♘xc3) **6...♗xe5 7 d4 ♗g7** *(51b)*, which looks quite satisfactory for Black, e.g. 8 ♗g5 f6, and then 9 ♗h4 0-0 (Motwani) is quite good for Black, who has several threats against White's uncoordinated pieces; 9 ♗f4 0-0 and again Black can be quite happy; or 9 ♗e3 0-0 with ideas of pushing the f-pawn.

In fact, no one has played 5 ♘xe5 in diagram 51a. In practice, the reply has always been 5 d4 exd4 6 ♘xd4 0-0 7 ♗e2 ♖e8 8 f3 c6! *(51c)*, reaching a position that arises more commonly from 1 c4 g6, and is discussed in Surprise No. 52. It is fully satisfactory for Black.

White only other way to proceed on move 5 is to go in for a slow Closed English, e.g. 5 g3 0-0 6 ♗g2, but with the knight on f3 rather than e2, his set-up is not very dangerous.

Surprise 52   B

Soundness: 3   Surprise Value: 3

Adorjan English

This is a related idea to the previous Surprise, but one that is a little better known. After **1 c4 g6** (considered by many King's Indian and Grünfeld players the most accurate), White can play **2 e4**, stopping the Grünfeld or Leningrad Dutch, and giving him more leeway against the Modern and King's Indian. Adorjan's idea is **2...e5!?** *(52a)*:

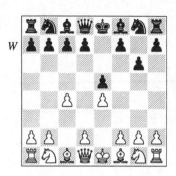

52a: after 2...e5

a) **3 ♘f3 ♗g7 4 d4** (otherwise a closed English results) **4...exd4 5 ♘xd4 ♘f6! 6 ♘c3** (6 e5 ♘e4!) **6...0-0 7 ♗e2 ♖e8 8 f3 c6!** is a position already seen in diagram 51c. It is like the King's Indian line 1 d4 ♘f6 2 c4 g6 3 ♘c3 ♗g7 4 e4 d6 5 ♘f3 0-0 6 ♗e2 e5 7 0-0 exd4 8 ♘xd4 ♖e8 9 f3 c6, except that Black can save a whole tempo by playing ...d7-d5 in one move, e.g. 9 ♘c2 d5 10 cxd5 cxd5 11 ♘xd5 ♘xd5 12 ♕xd5 ♕c7 *(52b)*

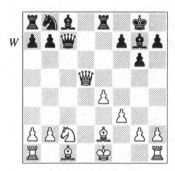

52b: after 12...♕c7

13 ♕c4 ♘c6 14 ♘e3 ♗e6 15 ♕c2 ♗e5 16 g3 ♗xg3+ 17 hxg3 ♕xg3+ 18 ♔d1 ♖ad8+ 19 ♗d2 ♘d4 is very good for Black, Santasiere-Marshall, New York 1941.

b) **3 d4** and now:

b1) **3...d6** is Surprise No. 64.

b2) **3...exd4 4 ♕xd4 f6!?** intending ...♘c6, ...♗g7, ...♘ge7, and ...f5 is suggested by Stohl.

b3) **3...♘f6 4 ♘f3** (4 dxe5 ♘xe4!; 4 ♘c3?! exd4 5 ♕xd4 ♘c6 6 ♕d2 ♗b4! puts White under pressure) **4...exd4 5 e5** *(52c)*

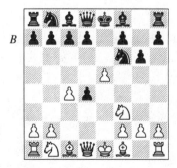

52c: after 5 e5

5...♗b4+ 6 ♗d2 ♕e7 7 ♗xb4 ♕xb4+ 8 ♕d2 ♕xd2+ (8...♕e7 is interesting) **9 ♘bxd2 ♘h5** (or 9...♘g8) **10 ♘xd4 ♘c6 11 ♘xc6 dxc6** is playable for Black.

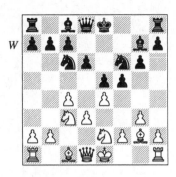

53a: after 7...♘f6

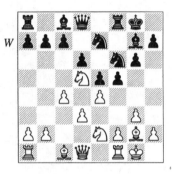

53b: after 9...♘e7

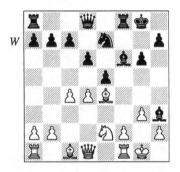

53c: after 12...♗h3

Surprise 53   *B*

Soundness: 3   Surprise Value: 2

English: Botvinnik 6...f5

Our key position can arise after the moves **1 c4 e5 2 ♘c3 ♘c6 3 g3 g6 4 ♗g2 ♗g7 5 e4 d6 6 ♘ge2 f5 7 d3 ♘f6** *(53a)*, but there are plenty of other move-orders that reach the position. If Black wishes to play a Closed English with ...e5, then there isn't much he can do to avoid the Botvinnik plan with e4. I recommend that Black delays moving his king's knight until he has played ...f5, thus reaching diagram 53a, which several new ideas are making quite attractive for Black:

a) **8 exf5 ♗xf5 9 h3 ♕d7 10 a3 0-0 11 ♗e3 ♖ae8 12 ♕d2 ♘d4 13 ♗xd4 exd4 14 ♘d5 ♘xd5 15 ♗xd5+ ♗e6 16 ♗g2 a6 17 g4 b5** gave Black the initiative in Sher-Sakaev, Dortmund 1992.

b) **8 h3 0-0 9 ♗e3 ♘h5 10 exf5 gxf5 11 ♘d5 f4!?** was OK for Black in Andersson-P.Nikolić, Tilburg 1987.

c) **8 0-0 0-0 9 ♘d5** (9 exf5 ♗xf5 10 h3 ♕d7 11 g4 ♗e6 12 ♘g3 h5!? 13 gxh5 gxh5 14 ♔h2 ♘d4 is clearly satisfactory for Black) **9...♘e7!** *(53b)* (Timman's new idea) **10 ♘xf6+** (10 ♗g5 c6 11 ♘xf6+ ♗xf6 12 ♗xf6 ♖xf6 is equal) **10...♗xf6** and then:

c1) **11 ♗e3 c6 12 ♖c1 ♗e6 13 f4 ♕d7 14 ♕d2 a6 15 b3 ♖ad8 16 ♗b6 ♖de8 17 ♗f2 fxe4 18 dxe4** led to a win for Black in Smejkal-Timman, Prague 1990.

c2) **11 d4** should be met by **11...fxe4!? 12 ♗xe4 ♗h3** *(53c)*.

c3) **11 ♗h6 ♖f7 12 ♕d2 c6 13 ♖ad1 ♗e6 14 b3 d5 15 exd5 cxd5 16 ♖fe1 ♕b6 17 ♘c3 ♖d8 18 ♗g5** is unclear, Makarychev-Yrjölä, Reykjavik 1990.

Surprise 54   *B*

Soundness: 4   Surprise Value: 3

Avoiding the King's Indian

The position after **1 ♘f3 ♘f6 2 g3 g6 3 ♗g2 ♗g7 4 0-0 0-0 5 d4 d6** can be reached via several move-orders. Many players are put off taking on the position as Black because after **6 c4** it seems the game has transposed to a main-line Fianchetto King's Indian. However, the **6...♗f5** *(54a)* idea we now consider is not available via a King's Indian move-order (with ♘c3 already played), and leads to play of a different type.

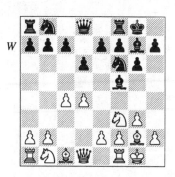

54a: after 6...♗f5

a) **7 ♘c3 ♘e4** (7...♕c8 is less good than in 'b', as White could play forcefully in the centre here) 8 ♘d5 (8 ♕b3 ♘xc3 gives Black an easy game) 8...c6 9 ♘e3 ♗d7 10 b3 (10 ♘d2 ♘xd2 forces 11 ♕xd2, compromising White's development) 10...f5 (a good Leningrad Dutch) 11 ♗b2 f4 12 ♘c2 ♘a6 *(54b)* 13 e3 fxg3 14 fxg3 ♕a5 15 ♘h4 ♘g5 16 ♕e1 ♘h3+ with the better game for Black, D.Walker-Sadler, British Ch (Hove) 1997.

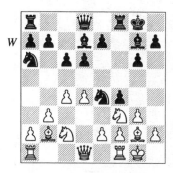

54b: after 12...♘a6

b) **7 b3 ♕c8 8 ♗b2** and now:

b1) **8...♗h3?!** 9 ♘c3 ♗xg2 10 ♔xg2 c5 11 d5 makes it hard for Black to find counterplay, Lechtynsky-Sznapik, Bratislava 1983.

b2) **8...♖e8** 9 ♘bd2 (9 ♘c3 e5) 9...c5 10 d5 a6 11 ♖e1 e5 12 ♘h4 e4!? 13 ♘f1 ♗h3 14 ♕d2 ♗xg2 15 ♔xg2 ♘bd7 16 f4 b5 is OK for Black, Bönsch-Romanishin, Lvov 1984.

b3) **8...♘a6!?** 9 ♘c3 c6 10 ♖e1 ♘e4 11 ♖c1 ♘xc3 12 ♗xc3 ♗e4 13 ♗f1 d5 *(54c)* 14 ♘d2 ♗f5 15 ♗g2 ♕d7 16 e3 ♖fe8 17 ♕e2 ♘c7 18 ♕f1 ♖ad8 19 h3 c5 is absolutely fine for Black, Rausis-Sadler, Hastings 1997/8.

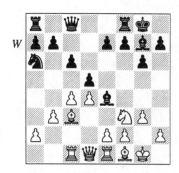

54c: after 13...d5

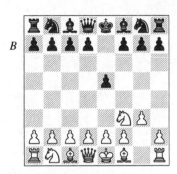

55a: after 2 ♘f3

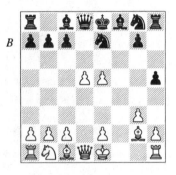

55b: after 9 dxe5

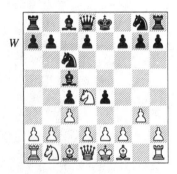

55c: after 6...♘c6

Surprise 55   *W*

Soundness: 2   Surprise Value: 4

Reversed Alekhine

It is not easy to get a good reversed Alekhine
Defence. **1 g3 e5 2 ♘f3** *(55a)* was condemned
by Alekhine on the basis of g3 being a
weakness in the reversed Chase Variation,
but there is very little practical experience.

a) **2...♘c6** 3 d4 e4 (3...exd4 4 ♘xd4 ♗c5
5 ♘b3 ♗b6 6 ♗g2 ±) 4 ♘e5 (4 d5 will be
equal; 4 ♘fd2 leads to reversed French positions where g3 isn't useful) 4...♘ce7 5 ♗g2
(5 d5 c6 6 ♘c3 isn't much of a winning attempt; 5 f3 d6 6 ♘g4 is the reverse of a line –
Surprise 49 – where g3 and ♗h3 would be
normal) 5...d5 (5...d6 6 ♘c4 d5 7 ♘e3 ±) 6
f3 h5 (6...f6 7 ♘g4 ♗xg4 8 fxg4) 7 fxe4 f6 8
exd5!? fxe5 9 dxe5 *(55b)* gives White three
good pawns for the piece.

b) **2...e4 3 ♘d4**:

b1) **3...d5** 4 d3 is a standard Alekhine reversed. g3 is useful and White can fight for
the advantage.

b2) **3...c5!** 4 ♘b3 c4 (4...d5 5 d3 f5 6
dxe4 fxe4 7 c4 d4 8 ♗g2 is treacherous for
Black) 5 ♘d4 (a reversed Chase Variation –
here g3 is of questionable value) 5...♗c5!
(5...♘c6 6 ♘xc6 dxc6 7 ♗g2 ♘f6 8 b3 cxb3
9 axb3 ♗c5 10 0-0 0-0 11 ♗b2 ♖e8 and
White has the better structure, but Black is
active, Chatalbashev-Radulski, Bulgarian Ch
1994) 6 c3 ♘c6 *(55c)* 7 ♘xc6 (7 ♘f5!?; 7 d3
exd3! is good for Black: 8 exd3 ♕e7+ or 8
♘xc6 dxc6! 9 exd3 ♕d5!) 7...dxc6 8 ♗g2
♘f6 9 b3 ♗e6 10 ♗a3 ♕e7 11 ♗xc5 ♕xc5
and White has problems activating his position, Mozes-Navrotescu, Romania 1993.

Surprise 56   *W*

Soundness: 3   Surprise Value: 5

English: Zviagintsev's 4 g4

One of the most remarkable novelties at FIDE's knockout 'world championship' was **1 c4 ♘f6 2 ♘f3 e6 3 ♘c3 ♗b4 4 g4** *(56a)*. This was used by the very strong, Dvoretsky-trained GM Zviagintsev in a critical play-off game, so the idea may be assumed to have some substance.

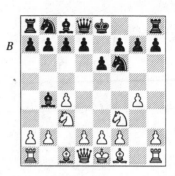

56a: after 4 g4

a) **4...♘xg4 5 ♖g1** is as yet untried. Then 5...♘h6 can be met by 6 ♖xg7 ♘f5, but maybe gambit play with 6 e4!? is the idea.

b) **4...d5** and then:

b1) **5 ♕a4+ ♘c6 6 ♘e5 ♕d6 7 ♘xc6** bxc6 is OK for Black.

b2) **5 g5 ♘e4 6 ♕a4+ ♘c6 7 ♘xe4 dxe4 8 ♘e5 e3 9 fxe3** *(56b)* 9...♕xg5 (after 9...♗d7 10 ♘xd7 ♕xg5, 11 ♘e5 ♕xe5 12 ♗g2 is annoying, e.g. 12...♕d6?? 13 a3 ♗c5 14 b4) 10 ♘f3 (10 ♘xc6?? ♗d7 11 ♕xb4 ♗xc6) 10...♕e7?! (now the b4-bishop is in danger) 11 a3 ♗d6 12 d4 ♗d7 13 ♕c2 ♕f6 14 b4 e5? 15 d5 ♗f5? 16 ♕a4! +− Krasenkow-Gild.Garcia, Groningen FIDE Wch 1997.

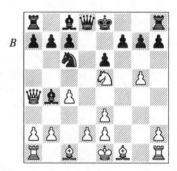

56b: after 9 fxe3

c) **4...h6 5 ♖g1 d6 6 h4** (6 ♕a4+ ♘c6 7 ♘d4 ♗xc3 8 ♘xc6 is inconsistent, and does not yield much) 6...e5 7 g5 hxg5 8 hxg5 ♘g4 9 ♘d5 ♗c5 10 d4 *(56c)* 10...♗b6 (10...exd4 11 b4 ±) 11 ♘xb6 (11 b4? e4!) 11...axb6 12 ♕d3 (targeting the g4-knight) 12...♘c6 13 ♕e4 f5! 14 gxf6 ♕xf6 15 dxe5 dxe5 16 ♖xg4 ♗f5 17 ♖h4 ♗xe4 18 ♖xh8+ ♔e7 19 ♗g5 (19 ♖xa8 ♗xf3 20 exf3 ♘d4 21 ♗d3 ♘xf3+ 22 ♔f1 ♘h2+ 23 ♔g2 ♕f3+ 24 ♔xh2 ♕xf2+ looks like a draw) 19...♖xh8 and Black has survived, Zviagintsev-Benjamin, Groningen FIDE Wch 1997.

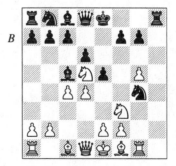

56c: after 10 d4

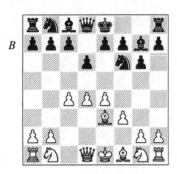

57a: after 5 f3

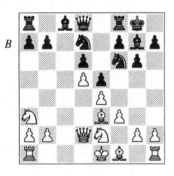

57b: after 10 ♘a3

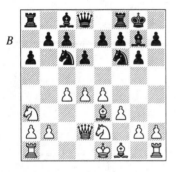

57c: after 8 ♘a3

Surprise 57   *W*

Soundness: 4   Surprise Value: 3

English: Pseudo-Sämisch

This line can arise when Black plays ...g6 against the English, viz. **1 c4 g6 2 e4 ♗g7 3 d4 d6 4 ♗e3 ♘f6 5 f3** *(57a)*, from a Modern (1 d4 g6 2 e4 ♗g7 3 c4 d6 4 ♗e3 ♘f6 5 f3), or via 1 d4 ♘f6 2 c4 g6 3 f3 ♗g7 4 e4 d6 5 ♗e3. A transposition to the Sämisch King's Indian will occur if White plays a quick ♘b1-c3 (probably the best reply to ...c5 ideas), but he can also keep the square free for the other knight, so as not to restrict his kingside development. The line is quite dangerous, with the added complication that however Black replies, he must also be ready to meet the analogous line of the regular Sämisch. Some examples after **5...0-0 6 ♘e2**:

a) **6....e5** 7 d5 c6 8 ♕d2 cxd5 9 cxd5 ♘bd7 10 ♘a3! *(57b)* 10...♘e8 11 ♘c3 f5 12 ♗e2 a6 13 0-0 f4?! 14 ♗f2 g5 15 b4 h5 16 ♘c4 ♖f6 17 a4 ♖g6 18 g4! gave White a significant positional advantage in Zsu.Polgar-Høi, Vejstrup 1989.

b) **6...♘c6** 7 ♕d2 a6 8 ♘a3 *(57c)* 8...♖b8 (8...e5?! 9 d5 ♘e7 10 c5 ♘e8 11 ♘c3 f5 12 ♗e2 f4 13 ♗f2 g5 14 0-0-0 ♘g6 15 ♘c4 ± Azmaiparashvili-Van Wely, Amsterdam 1989) 9 ♖c1 ♘e8 10 c5 (Gausel suggests 10 b4 intending b5) 10...f5 (10...d5?! 11 exd5 ♕xd5 12 ♘c3 ±) 11 exf5 ♗xf5 12 d5! ♘e5 13 ♘f4 dxc5 14 ♖xc5 ♘d6 15 ♗e2 ♗d7! 16 ♘e6 ♗xe6 17 dxe6 ♘f5! 18 ♗f4! ♘c6 (18...♕xd2+ 19 ♗xd2 and ♗c3 ±) 19 ♖d5! ♕c8 20 ♖d7 ♘e5 (Agdestein-Djurhuus, Hammerfest 1993) and here Djurhuus indicated 21 ♗xe5 ♗xe5 22 ♘c4 ♗f6 as good for White.

Surprise 58   *B*

Soundness: 4   Surprise Value: 3

Wahls's Anti-KIA/Réti idea

·1 ♘f3 ♘f6 2 g3 g6 3 ♗g2 ♗g7 4 0-0 0-0 5 d3 is quite an annoying line for Black to play against. White resolutely refuses to take Black on in a King's Indian or Grün-feld, and after 5...d6 will angle for a Closed Sicilian with 6 e4 or an English with 6 c4. Wahls's idea is **5...d5** *(58a)*, which has some nice and surprising points, the main one being to meet 6 ♘bd2 with 6...d4!, and then after 7 e4 to take *en passant*. That position is discussed in the next Surprise. Here we deal with the alternatives:

a) **6 a3** b6 7 b4 ♗b7 8 ♗b2 c5 9 ♘bd2 ♘bd7 is rock-solid for Black, e.g. 10 ♖b1 ♕c7 11 bxc5 bxc5 12 ♘e5 ♘b6 13 ♗a1 ♖ad8 14 e3 ♘e8 15 f4 ♘d6 16 ♕e1 (Dizdarević-Uhlmann, Sarajevo 1981) 16...f6 ∓ Uhlmann.

b) **6 c3** ♘c6 (6...a5!?) 7 ♘bd2 (7 b4 a6) 7...e5 is fine for Black, since any attempt by White to play in KIA style with e4 is ineffective with him having wasted time and weakened the a6-f1 diagonal by the move c3.

c) **6 ♘bd2 d4!?** 7 ♘c4 (7 a4 ♘d5 8 ♘c4 c5 transposes) **7...c5 8 a4** (8 e4 b5 9 ♘cd2 ♗b7 10 ♕e2 ♘c6 11 e5 ♘d5 Speckner-Wahls, Bundesliga 1986/7) **8...♘d5** *(58b)* and then:

c1) **9 e4** dxe3 (the standard theme) 10 ♘xe3 ♘c6 11 c3 e6 12 ♖e1 ♘ce7 is OK for Black, Moingt-Avrukh, European Clubs Cup 1996.

c2) **9 ♘fd2** ♘c6 10 e4 dxe3 11 fxe3 b6 12 ♕f3 ♗e6 13 ♘e4 h6 *(58c)* gave Black quite an attractive position in Hug-Wahls, Bern Z 1990.

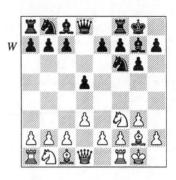

58a: after 5...d5

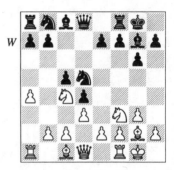

58b: after 8...♘d5

58c: after 13...h6

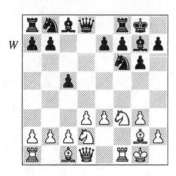

59a: after 8...c5

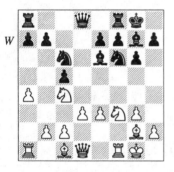

59b: after 10...♗e6

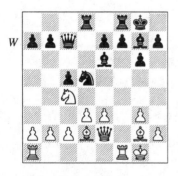

59c: after 14...♘d5

Surprise 59   *B*

Soundness: 3   Surprise Value: 4

Wahls's idea: Main line

After **1 ♘f3 ♘f6 2 g3 g6 3 ♗g2 ♗g7 4 0-0 0-0 5 d3 d5 6 ♘bd2 d4!**, most players, I imagine, will play **7 e4** and be surprised by the answer **7...dxe3! 8 fxe3 c5** *(59a)*. Indeed, it seems illogical for Black to make three moves with his d-pawn and, apparently, have nothing to show for it. However, it now turns out to be very difficult for White to get his pieces and centre pawns (which have no 'ideal formation' to advance into) working together without leaving weaknesses:

  a) **9 ♘c4 ♘c6 10 a4 ♗e6** *(59b)*, planning to make White's pawns really weak by taking on c4, gives Black a good position, as Wahls's analysis shows: 11 b3 ♘d5; 11 ♘a3 ♕d7; 11 ♘ce5 ♘xe5 12 ♘xe5 ♕c7; or 11 ♕e2 ♗xc4 12 dxc4 ♘d7 13 ♖b1 ♕a5 14 b3 ♖ad8 15 ♗d2 ♕c7.

  b) **9 ♕e2 ♘c6 10 ♘c4 ♗e6 11 ♘fe5** (for 11 a4 see line 'a') 11...♘xe5 12 ♘xe5 ♕c7 13 ♘c4 (13 ♘f3 is met by 13...c4, when White's pawns will be weakened one way or another) 13...♖ad8 (13...♗xc4!? would not be at all bad for Black either) 14 ♗d2 ♘d5 *(59c)* 15 e4?! (the centralized knight is annoying, but this move blocks off the g2-bishop; Wahls notes 15 c3?! b5, and suggests 15 a3) 15...♘b4 16 ♗f4 ♕c8 17 a3 ♘c6 18 c3 h6 (planning 19...b5, when 20 ♘e3 would trap the f4-bishop) 19 h4 ♗g4 20 ♗f3 ♗h3 21 ♖fd1 b5 22 ♘d2 ♘e5 23 ♗xe5 ♗xe5 was obviously good for Black in Wittke-Wahls, Berlin 1989.

Surprise 60   W

Soundness: 3   Surprise Value: 5

Reversed Fajarowicz

If you like the type of play Black gets in the Fajarowicz Gambit, then there is a way to get an improved version as White: **1 ♘f3 d5** (or 1...c5 2 b3 d5) **2 b3 c5 3 e4!?** *(60a)*. In the positions that result, b3 is a very useful move indeed. If you are thinking that Black playing such an early ...c5 is a bit cooperative, consider that 1...c5 will be the choice of many Sicilian players, while 1 ♘f3 d5 2 b3 c5 3 ♗b2 f6 was once used by Fischer to crush Petrosian. On to specifics:

a) **3...d4?!** 4 ♗c4.

b) **3...♘f6** can be met by 4 exd5 ♘xd5 5 ♗b2 or 4 e5 ♘fd7 5 e6!? fxe6 6 ♗b2, a pawn sacrifice to disrupt Black's game.

c) **3...e6** is known via 1 e4 c5 2 ♘f3 e6 3 b3 d5. One idea is 4 exd5 exd5 5 ♗b2 *(60b)*, e.g. 5...♘f6 6 ♗b5+ ♘c6 (6...♗d7 7 ♕e2+ and 8 ♗xf6) 7 ♘e5 ♕d6 8 0-0 ♗e7 9 d4 ± Novopashin-Kirpichnikov, Rostov 1975.

d) **3...dxe4 4 ♘e5** *(60c)* with the following sample possibilities:

d1) **4...♕d4?** 5 ♗b2 ♕xb2 6 ♘c3 traps the queen (6...♕a3 7 ♗b5+!; 6...♕e6 7 a3).

d2) **4...♕c7** 5 ♗b2 ♘f6 6 ♗b5+ ♗d7 7 ♘xd7 ♘bxd7 8 ♕e2 a6 9 ♗xd7+ ♕xd7 10 ♘c3 and it is risky for Black to try to hold on to the pawn, e.g. 10...♕c6 11 0-0-0 ♖d8 12 ♖he1 ♖d4 13 g4 h6 14 h4.

d3) **4...♘f6** 5 ♗b5+ ♘bd7 (5...♗d7) 6 ♕e2 a6 7 ♗xd7+ ♗xd7 8 ♘c3 ♗f5 9 ♗b2 ♕c7 10 ♘c4 b5 11 ♘e3.

d4) **4...a6** (cf. Surprise 94) 5 ♗b2 ♘f6 6 a4 ♘bd7 7 ♘c4 b6 8 ♕e2 ♗b7 9 ♘c3 e6 10 0-0-0 ♗e7 11 ♖g1 intending g4.

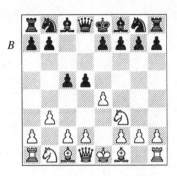

60a: after 3 e4

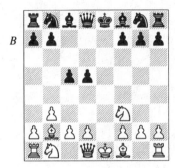

60b: after 5 ♗b2

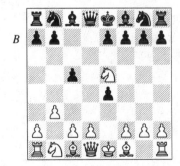

60c: after 5 ♘e5

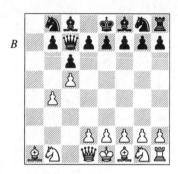

61a: after 7 ♗xa1

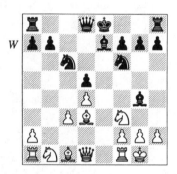

61b: after 9...♘f6

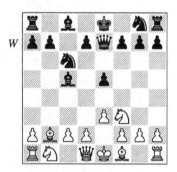

61c: after 5...♕e7

Surprise 61   *B*

Soundness: 3   Surprise Value: 3

Anti-Sokolsky ideas

Here we consider two lines for Black against the Sokolsky Opening, **1 b4**:

a) **1...c6** and then:

a1) **2 ♗b2 ♕b6!** (avoiding the messy gambit 2...a5 3 b5 cxb5 4 e3 b4 5 a3) 3 a3 a5 4 c4 axb4 5 c5 ♕c7 6 axb4 ♖xa1 7 ♗xa1 *(61a)* is a position claimed in some theory books to favour White. However, when it occurred in actual play, Black easily got a very pleasant game by 7...d6 8 ♕a4 e5 9 ♘f3 ♘d7 10 cxd6 ♗xd6 11 g3 ♘gf6, Teichmann-Watts, British Ch (Southampton) 1986.

a2) **2 c4** d5 3 e3 e5 4 ♗b2 f6 5 a3 ♗e6 6 cxd5 cxd5 7 d4 e4 8 ♘e2 f5 9 ♘f4 ♗f7 10 h4 ♘f6 11 ♘c3 ♗d6 12 ♕b3 ♘bd7 gave Black a solid space advantage in Sjöberg-Rõtšagov, Gothenburg 1997.

b) **1...c5!?** **2 bxc5** (2 b5 d5; 2 e4?! is a Sicilian Wing Gambit) **2...e5 3 ♗b2** (3 e3 ♗xc5 4 d4 exd4 5 exd4 ♗e7 6 ♗d3 d5 7 ♘f3 ♘c6 8 0-0 ♗g4 9 c3 ♘f6 *(61b)* gave Black an entirely respectable position in Katalymov-Kupreichik, Minsk 1971) **3...♘c6 4 ♘f3 ♗xc5** (threatening ...♕b6) **5 e3** (5 ♘xe5? ♗xf2+ 6 ♔xf2 ♕b6+ wins material; 5 ♗xe5? ♘xe5 6 ♘xe5 ♗d4 picks up at least an exchange; 5 d4? ♕b6 leaves White in a mess) and now:

b1) **5...f6?!** 6 ♗e2 d5 7 0-0 d4 8 exd4 ♘xd4 9 ♘xd4 ♗xd4 10 c3 ♗b6 11 d4 broke open the position to White's advantage in Sveshnikov-Pantaleev, Khavirov 1968.

b2) **5...♕e7** *(61c)* 6 ♗b5 f6 7 0-0 a6 8 ♗c4 b5 9 ♗d5 ♕d6 (Palme) is playable for Black.

Surprise 62 B

Soundness: 2 Surprise Value: 4

English: Myers Defence

Here we turn our attention to **1 c4 g5** *(62a)*.
No, this is not an attack of Basmania (...g5
and ...h6 against anything), but rather an attempt to profit from a drawback of White's
first move: that he can no longer fortify the
long diagonal by c2-c3. This means that it is
difficult for White to threaten $\triangle$c1xg5 in
earnest. Meanwhile the pawn stakes out
space on the kingside and is ready to kick a
knight from f3 by ...g4. If White replies very
quietly, normal-looking positions can be
reached, but where Black has gained a tempo
for his kingside play by playing ...g7-g5
rather than ...g7-g6-g5.

On the other hand, 1...g5 is a grotesque
weakening of Black's kingside, and highly
inventive play is needed for Black to stay on
the board at all. Such play is frequently seen
in the games of the Finnish player, Kari Hei-
nola, who has played 1...g5 many times with
great virtuosity. If you wish to try this line, I
recommend a careful study of his ideas.

a) **2 h4** gxh4 3 $\triangle$f3 h3 4 g3 d5 5 $\triangle$xh3
$\triangle$xh3 6 Ξxh3 dxc4 7 $\mathbb{W}$a4+ $\mathbb{W}$d7 = Tuomai-
nen-Heinola, Finland 1985.

b) **2 e4** c5 (2...$\triangle$g7 3 h4 gxh4 4 $\mathbb{W}$g4 is
annoying) 3 d4 $\triangle$g7 4 dxc5 $\triangle$c6 5 $\triangle$c3
$\triangle$xc3+ 6 bxc3 *(62b)* and now 6...$\triangle$f6 looks
right.

c) **2 d3** h6 (...h6 is reasonable when
White has played something slow) 3 e4 c5 4
$\triangle$e2 $\triangle$c6 5 $\triangle$g3 d6 6 $\triangle$e2 e5 7 0-0 $\triangle$ge7 8
$\triangle$c3 $\triangle$g6 9 $\triangle$g4 $\triangle$e6 10 $\triangle$d5 $\triangle$g7 11 $\triangle$h5
0-0 12 $\triangle$f5 $\triangle$d4 = Kauko-Heinola, Tam-
pere 1990.

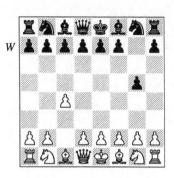

62a: after 1...g5

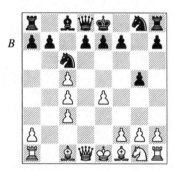

62b: after 6 bxc3

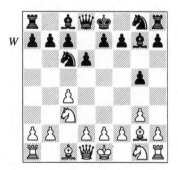

62c: after 4...$\triangle$c6

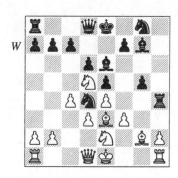

62d: after 11...♘d4

62e: after 9...h5

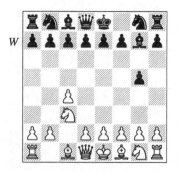

62f: after 2...♗g7

d) **2 g3 d6 3 ♗g2 ♗g7 4 ♘c3 ♘c6** (*62c*) is White's 'slow play' option:

d1) **5 e4 e5 6 d3 h5 7 ♘ge2 h4 8 gxh4 ♖xh4 9 ♘d5 ♗g4 10 f3 ♗e6 11 ♗e3 ♘d4** (*62d*) **12 ♘xd4 exd4 13 ♗f2 ♖h8 14 ♘b4 ♘e7 15 ♕b3 c5 16 ♘d5 ♗xd5 17 cxd5 ♕a5+ 18 ♔f1 0-0-0** with a nice game for Black, Haataja-Heinola, Finnish open Ch (Vantaa) 1988.

d2) **5 e3 e5 6 ♘ge2 f5 7 d3 ♘f6 8 ♖b1 a5 9 a3 h5** (*62e*) (this looks like a normal English, with accelerated kingside play for Black) **10 b4 axb4 11 axb4 h4 12 ♘d5 ♘xd5 13 cxd5 h3 14 ♗f1 ♘e7** ∓ Bogø-G.Welling, Lyngby 1990.

d3) **5 d3 g4** (unless it is too weakening, this the preferred way of dealing with the attack on the g5-pawn – especially when White has played g3 since ...h5-h4 may be a good follow-up) **6 h3 h5 7 ♗g5 ♘f6 8 e3 ♘e5 9 d4 ♘g6 10 ♘ge2 c6 11 ♘f4 ♕a5** is OK for Black, Kauko-Heinola, Tampere 1991.

e) **2 ♘c3 ♗g7** (*62f*):

e1) **3 b3 d6 4 ♗b2 ♘c6 5 e3 e5 6 ♘ge2 ♗g4 7 h3 ♗h5 8 g4 ♗g6 9 ♘g3 ♘h6 10 d3 f5** with activity, Paldanius-Heinola, Finland 1984.

e2) **3 e4 d6 4 d3 g4 5 ♗e3 e5 6 ♕d2 ♘c6 7 ♘ge2 h5 8 ♘d5 ♘d4 9 ♗xd4 exd4 10 g3 c6 11 ♘df4 h4 12 ♗g2 h3 13 ♗f1 ♕b6 14 ♘c1 ♗h6 15 ♗e2 ♘e7 16 f3 ♘g6** ∓ Linqvist-Heinola, Finnish open Ch (Espoo) 1985.

e3) **3 g3 d6 4 d3 g4 5 h3 h5 6 hxg4 hxg4 7 ♖xh8 ♗xh8 8 ♕d2 c6 9 ♕g5 ♗xc3+ 10 bxc3 ♘f6 11 ♖b1 ♔d7 12 e4 ♕g8 13 ♕f5+ ♔c7 14 ♕a5+ b6 15 ♕a3 ♘bd7** with a respectable position for Black, Kivipelto-Heinola, Helsinki 1990.

The main line, 2 d4, is discussed in the next Surprise.

Surprise 63   *B*

Soundness: 2   Surprise Value: 4

English, Myers: 2 d4

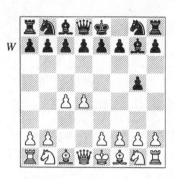

After **1 c4 g5 2 d4 ♗g7** *(63a)* there are:

a) **3 e3** c5 4 d5 d6 5 ♗d3 ♘d7 6 ♘e2 ♘e5 7 ♘g3 ♕a5+ 8 ♔f1 (Koskinen-Heinola, Tampere 1992) 8...♘f6 is unclear.

63a: after 2...♗g7

b) **3 e4** c5 4 ♘e2 cxd4 5 ♘xd4 ♘c6 6 ♘xc6 bxc6 is OK for Black, Haila-Heinola, Finland 1987

c) **3 ♗xg5 c5** and then:

c1) After **4 ♘f3** *(63b)*, **4...♕b6** 5 ♘bd2 (5 ♘c3 ♕xb2) 5...cxd4 6 ♘b3 e5, Zander-Leisebein, corr. 1988, and **4...cxd4** 5 ♕b3 (5 ♘xd4 ♕b6 ∓) 5...♘c6 6 ♘bd2 d6 are both messy, Haapaniemi-Heinola, Järvenpää 1985.

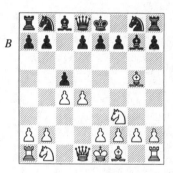

c2) **4 e3** ♕a5+ 5 ♕d2 (not 5 ♘c3?? cxd4) 5...♕xd2+ 6 ♘xd2 cxd4 7 exd4 ♗xd4 8 ♖b1 ♘c6 is unclear – G.Welling.

63b: after 4 ♘f3

d) **3 ♘c3 g4** (3...c5 4 dxc5 h6 5 ♗e3 ♘c6 6 ♘f3 ♕a5 7 ♕d2 ♘f6 8 ♘d5 ± Benjamin-Heinola, Hawaii 1996) **4 e4** (4 ♗f4 d6 5 g3 ♘c6 6 d5 e5 ∓ Slavin-Faldon, corr 1981; 4 e3 d6 5 ♘ge2 ♘c6 6 ♘f4 h5 7 g3 e5 8 dxe5 ♘xe5 ∓ Haila-Heinola, Finland 1984; 4 ♗g5 c5 5 d5 ♗xc3+ 6 bxc3 ♕a5 is OK for Black, Issakainen-Heinola, Järvenpää 1985) **4...d6** *(63c)* and now:

d1) **5 ♗e2** h5 6 h3 ♘c6 7 ♗e3 e5 8 d5 ♘d4 = Hillila-Heinola, Tampere 1987.

d2) **5 ♘ge2** ♘c6 6 ♗e3 e5 7 d5 (7 ♕d2 – see 5 ♗e3) 7...♘ce7 8 ♘g3 h5 9 ♗d3 ♘g6 10 ♘f5 ♗xf5 11 exf5 ♘h4 12 ♗e4 (Keto-Heinola, Pori Ch 1984) and now 12...♕d7 looks quite all right for Black.

d3) **5 ♗e3** ♘c6 6 ♕d2 e5 7 ♘ge2 f5 8 dxe5 ♗xe5 9 exf5 ♗xf5 10 ♘g3 ♘ge7 11 ♗e2 ± Aaltio-Heinola, Helsinki 1985.

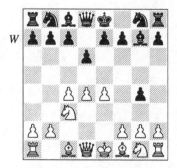

63c: after 4...d6

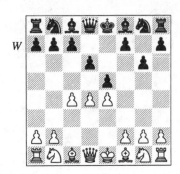

64a: after 3...e5

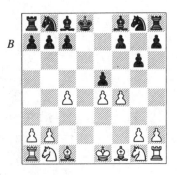

64b: after 6 f4

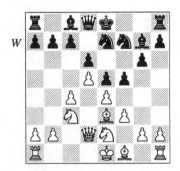

64c: after 9...♘f7

Surprise 64   *B*

Soundness: 3   Surprise Value: 3

A More Palatable Modern

One of the practical drawbacks to playing the Modern is that after 1 d4 g6 2 e4 ♗g7 3 c4 d6 4 ♘c3, the natural 4...e5 can be met by 5 dxe5 dxe5 6 ♕xd8+ ♔xd8 7 f4. Although this isn't necessarily too unpleasant for Black, it is deadly dull and kills Black's winning chances. **1 d4 g6 2 e4 d6 3 c4 e5** *(64a)* (or these moves in some other order) aims for an improved version. Now if White exchanges queens, the black bishop will be able to find a better square than g7: either h6, to exchange off the now 'bad' bishop, or an active post on c5 or b4. Some variations:

a) **4 dxe5 dxe5 5 ♕xd8+ ♔xd8 6 f4** *(64b)* **6...♗h6!?** (6...♗b4+ 7 ♘c3 ♘f6 is perfectly OK too) **7 g3 ♘f6 8 ♘c3 ♖e8 9 fxe5 ♗xc1 10 ♖xc1 ♘g4 11 ♖d1+ ♗d7 12 e6! fxe6 13 ♗e2 ♘e5 14 ♘f3 ♘bc6 15 ♘b5 ♘xf3+ 16 ♗xf3 ♘e5 17 ♗e2 ♖f8 18 ♖f1 ♖xf1+ 19 ♔xf1 ♔e7!** with at least equality, Fedder-D.Cramling, Helsingborg tt 1990.

b) **4 ♘e2 ♘c6 5 ♘bc3 ♗g7 6 ♗e3 ♘h6** (6...f5!?) **7 f3 f5 8 d5** (after 8 ♕d2 Black has various options, but 8...exd4!? 9 ♘xd4 f4 looks very interesting) **8...♘e7 9 ♕d2 ♘f7** *(64c)* and then:

b1) **10 c5 h5!?**.

b2) **10 0-0-0** 0-0 (10...h5!?) **11 ♔b1 c5 12 dxc6 bxc6 13 c5** is maybe a shade better for White, Šahović-Todorčević, Yugoslavia 1981.

b3) **10 g3 c5 11 ♗g2 h5 12 0-0 h4 13 ♖ae1 a6 14 b3 ♗d7 15 ♘c1 ♕a5 16 ♘d3 f4 17 gxf4 exf4** with good play for Black, Ermenkov-Azmaiparashvili, Burgas 1994.

c) **4 ♘f3** and then:

c1) **4...♘c6** 5 d5 ♘ce7 6 h4 ♘f6 (6...f5!?) 7 ♘c3 ♗g7 8 ♗g5 0-0 9 ♗e2 ♘h5 10 g3 f5 is unclear – King.

c2) **4...exd4** 5 ♕xd4 (5 ♘xd4 will transpose to main variations of the Modern – if that doesn't suit Black, he shouldn't play 4...exd4) 5...♘f6 6 ♗g5 ♗g7 *(64d)* 7 e5 dxe5 8 ♕xe5+ ♔f8 9 ♘c3 h6 10 ♗f4 ♘a6 11 ♖d1 ♕e8 12 ♗e2 g5 13 ♕xe8+ ♘xe8 and Black is through the worst, Situru-Hickl, Jakarta 1996.

c3) **4...♗g4** 5 d5 ♘d7 6 ♘bd2 ♘gf6 7 h3 ♗xf3 8 ♕xf3 h5 9 h4 ♗h6 shouldn't be too bad for Black, Knaak-S.Mohr, Bad Lauterberg 1991.

d) **4 ♘c3** exd4 5 ♕xd4 ♘f6 6 ♗g5 ♘bd7 7 f4 (7 0-0-0 h6 8 ♗f4 ♗g7 9 ♕d2 g5 10 ♗e3 ♘g4 = Bagaturov-Nogueiras, Biel IZ 1993) 7...h6 8 ♗h4 c5 9 ♕d3 g5 *(64e)* 10 fxg5 ♘g4 11 ♘f3 ♘de5 12 ♕d2 ♗e7 13 0-0-0 ♗e6 14 ♘b5 hxg5 15 ♗g3 f6 16 b3 (16 ♘xd6+ ♗xd6 17 ♕xd6 ♕xd6 18 ♖xd6 ♔e7 19 ♘xe5 ♘xe5 20 ♗xe5 fxe5 21 ♖d2 ♖af8 and Black's far better bishop compensates for the pawn) 16...♘f7 17 ♗e2 (17 ♘xd6+ ♗xd6 18 ♗xd6 ♘xd6 19 ♕xd6 ♕xd6 20 ♖xd6 ♘f2 21 ♖g1 ♔e7 22 ♖d2 ♘xe4 ∓) 17...♕b6 18 h3 ♘ge5 19 ♘xe5 dxe5 20 ♗f3 ♖d8 21 ♕c2 a6 22 ♘c3 ♕a5 ½-½ Hort-Hickl, German Ch 1991.

e) **4 d5** gives Black a wide range of options, which his move-order, without ...♗g7, has only served to enhance.

f) **4 ♗e3** ♘c6 5 ♘e2 ♘h6 6 f3 f5 7 d5 ♘e7 8 ♕d2 ♘f7 *(64f)* 9 ♘ec3 (the same flexible use of the knights as we saw in Surprise 57) 9...♘g8 10 ♗d3 ♗h6 11 exf5 ♗xe3 12 ♕xe3 gxf5 13 ♘d2 with a modest edge for White, Panno-Suttles, Palma de Mallorca IZ 1970.

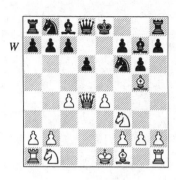

64d: after 6...♗g7

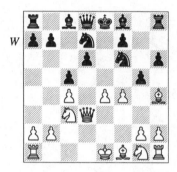

64e: after 9...g5

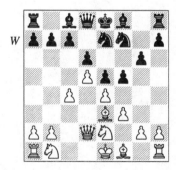

64f: after 8...♘f7

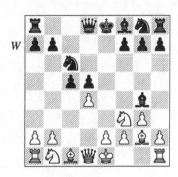

65a: after 6...♗g4

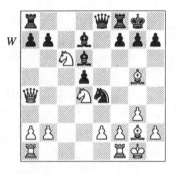

65b: after 14...♘e4

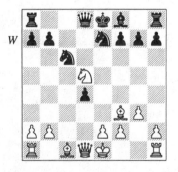

65c: after 9...♘ge7

Surprise 65   B

Soundness: 2   Surprise Value: 4

QGD Tarrasch: quick ...♗g4

This rare and forgotten side-variation in the Tarrasch can make a useful surprise weapon, and can be used whether White has played 3 ♘f3 or 3 ♘c3. After **1 d4 d5 2 c4 e6 3 ♘f3** (3 ♘c3 c5 4 cxd5 exd5 5 ♘f3 ♘c6 6 g3 ♗g4 generally transposes after 7 ♗g2 to line 'd', while 7 dxc5 d4 8 ♘e4 isn't too fearsome) **3...c5 4 cxd5 exd5 5 g3 ♘c6 6 ♗g2 ♗g4** *(65a)* White can play:

a) **7 ♗e3** c4 8 ♘e5 ♗b4+ 9 ♘c3 ♗e6 10 0-0 ♘ge7 11 ♘xc6 ♘xc6 is similar to the Swedish Variation, but the white bishop is misplaced on e3, blocking the e-pawn, Spacek-Bezold, Berlin 1990.

b) **7 0-0** ♘f6 8 ♘e5 ♗e6 9 ♕a4 cxd4 10 ♘d2 ♗d6 11 ♘df3 0-0 12 ♘xc6 ♕e8 13 ♘fxd4 ♗d7 14 ♗g5 ♘e4 *(65b)* 15 ♗e7 ♗xc6 16 ♘xc6 ♗xe7 17 ♘xe7+ ♕xe7 18 ♕d4 ± Wells-Bezold, Budapest 1993.

c) **7 ♘e5** ♗e6 8 ♘xc6 bxc6 9 dxc5 ♗xc5 10 ♕c2 ♕b6 isn't too bad for Black, Furman-Kholmov, USSR Ch (Kiev) 1954.

d) **7 ♘c3 ♗xf3 8 ♗xf3 cxd4 9 ♘xd5 ♘ge7** *(65c)* is a critical position:

d1) **10 ♕b3** ♘xd5 11 ♗xd5 ♗b4+ 12 ♔f1 ♕e7 is playable for Black, Burgess-Sv.Johnsen, Gausdal Troll 1991.

d2) **10 e4** dxe3 11 ♗xe3 ♘xd5 12 ♕xd5 ♗b4+ 13 ♔f1 ♕f6 ± Bondarevsky-Mikenas, USSR 1958.

d3) **10 ♘f4** g6 11 0-0 ♗g7 12 ♘d3 0-0 13 ♗g5, ± Mikenas, but can this really be so bad after 13...♕b6?

Surprise 66   W

Soundness: 3   Surprise Value: 2

Semi-Slav, 7 a4 ♕b6 with d5

Our theme position here arises if White tries the aggressive line **1 d4 d5 2 c4 c6 3 ♘f3 ♘f6 4 ♘c3 e6 5 ♗g5 dxc4 6 e4 b5 7 a4** and Black replies with the equally combative **7...♕b6**. White's consistent follow-up is then **8 ♗xf6 gxf6 9 ♗e2** *(66a)*. The new and surprising treatment for White involves a very quick d4-d5 advance, normally as soon as the c8-bishop fails to cover the e6-pawn, e.g.:

a) **9...a6** – see the next Surprise.

b) **9...♘d7** 10 d5 b4 (10...♗b4 11 dxc6 ♕xc6 12 ♘d4 ♕xe4 13 0-0 ±) 11 a5 (the standard reply to ...b4) 11...♕c7 12 dxe6 fxe6 13 ♘a4 ♘e5 14 ♘xe5 ♕xe5 15 0-0 is good for White, Vakhidov-Galakhov, Tashkent 1984.

c) **9...♗b4** 10 d5! ♗b7 11 dxe6 fxe6 12 0-0 *(66b)* 12...♘a6 (12...0-0 13 ♘a2 ♖d8 14 ♕c2 ♗e7 15 e5 gives White nice play, e.g. 15...f5?! 16 b3 cxb3 17 ♕xb3 – Soln) 13 e5 f5 14 ♕d4! (the queen is holding together Black's queenside) 14...♘c7 (14...♕xd4 15 ♘xd4) 15 ♕h4 with an attack, Soln-Sulava, Bled 1995.

d) **9...♗b7 10 d5** and then:

d1) **10...cxd5** 11 exd5 b4 12 a5 ♕c7 13 a6!? *(66c)* (exploiting Black's omission of ...a6) 13...♗xa6 14 ♘e4 ♕f4 (14...f5? 15 ♕a4+ ♔d8 16 d6 ♕b6 17 ♘e5) 15 ♖xa6 ♕xe4 (15...♘xa6 16 ♕a4+ ♔d8 17 ♕xa6) 16 ♕a4+ ♔d8 (16...♘d7 17 dxe6) 17 ♖xa7 with good attacking chances.

d2) **10...b4** 11 dxe6 fxe6 (11...bxc3 12 exf7+) 12 a5 ♕c7 13 ♘a4 c5 (13...♖g8!?) 14 ♗xc4 ♕c6 15 0-0 ♖g8 16 ♖e1 ± Burgess-Thorsteinsson, Gausdal Eikrem mem 1997.

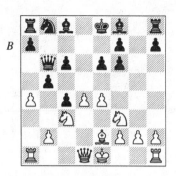

66a: after 9 ♗e2

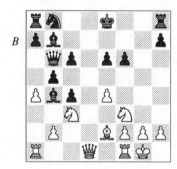

66b: after 12 0-0

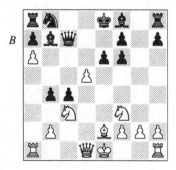

66c: after 13 a6

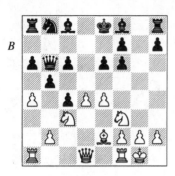

67a: after 10 0-0

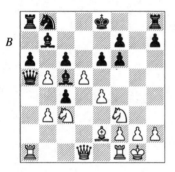

67b: after 13 axb5

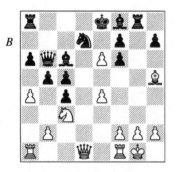

67c: after 15 dxe6

Surprise 67   W

Soundness: 3   Surprise Value: 2

Semi-Slav, 7 a4 ♕b6 (2)

After **1 d4 d5 2 c4 c6 3 ♘f3 ♘f6 4 ♘c3 e6 5 ♗g5 dxc4 6 e4 b5 7 a4 ♕b6 8 ♗xf6 gxf6 9 ♗e2**, Black's most common move is **9...a6**, which should be met by **10 0-0** (*67a*) and then after most replies d5:

a) **10...♘d7** 11 d5 ♖b8 (11...♘c5 12 ♕d4 ♗e7 13 dxc6 b4 14 ♘d5 exd5 15 exd5 ± Tukmakov-Machulsky, USSR 1982) 12 dxc6 ♕xc6 13 axb5 axb5 14 ♘d4 ± Garcia-Santos, 1976.

b) **10...♖a7** (with ideas of ...♖d7) 11 b3 b4 12 a5 ♕d8 13 ♘a4 c3 14 ♘b6 ♘d7 (or 14...♗b7 15 ♗c4 and d5) 15 ♘xc8 ♕xc8 16 d5 with a big initiative, Lukacs-Hölzl, Budapest 1987.

c) **10...♗b7 11 d5** and then:

c1) **11...b4** is met by the thematic sacrifice 12 dxe6 fxe6 (12...bxc3? 13 exf7+ starts a decisive attack) 13 a5 with ♘a4 to follow.

c2) **11...♘c5** 12 b3 (logical, since ...♗b4 would now cost a tempo) 12...♕a5 (12...cxb3 13 dxe6 and ♕xb3) 13 axb5! (*67b*) 13...♕xc3 14 bxc6 ♘xc6 15 ♖c1 gives Black problems with his clutter of pieces on the c-file.

c3) **11...cxd5** 12 exd5 b4 (12...♘d7 13 axb5 axb5 14 ♖xa8+ ♗xa8 15 ♘d4 ♗c5 16 ♘dxb5 ♘e5 17 b3 ± – safer king) 13 a5 ♕c7 14 dxe6!? bxc3 15 ♘d4 ♖g8 16 ♕a4+ ♔d8 17 g3 ♗d5 18 ♖fd1 ♔c8 (Tal-Keller, Zurich 1959) 19 ♕e8+! +–.

c4) **11...♘d7** 12 ♘d4! c5?! (12...cxd5 13 exd5) 13 ♘c6 ♖g8 (13...♗xc6 14 dxc6 ♕xc6 15 axb5) 14 ♗h5 ♗xc6?! 15 dxe6! (*67c*) gave White a winning attack in Bellon-Antunes, Platja d'Aro 1994.

Surprise 68 W

Soundness: 4 Surprise Value: 3

Semi-Slav: Ragozin Gambit

Many years ago Ragozin introduced the following exchange sacrifice: **1 d4 ♞f6 2 c4 e6 3 ♞f3 d5 4 ♞c3 c6 5 ♝g5 dxc4 6 e4 b5 7 e5 h6 8 ♝h4 g5 9 ♞xg5 ♞d5 10 ♞xf7 ♛xh4 11 ♞xh8 ♝b4** *(68a)*. It has never been very respectable, but nor has it been completely refuted.

Since the lines 12 ♖c1 c5 13 dxc5 ♛g5!? and 12 ♛d2 c5 13 0-0-0 ♞c6 14 ♞g6 ♝xc3 15 bxc3 ♛e4!? (e.g. 16 ♛xh6 ♞xc3 17 ♛f8+ ♚d7 18 ♝xc4 ♛b1+ 19 ♚d2 ♛b2+ 20 ♚e1 ♚c7!) don't seem clear, I advocate an idea introduced by Hannes Stefansson: **12 a3!? ♞xc3 13 ♛f3!** *(68b)*. Then:

a) **13...♞e4+** 14 axb4 ♞g5 15 ♛f8+ ♚xf8 16 ♞g6+ extricates the knight, and keeps an extra exchange.

b) **13...♞d5+** 14 axb4 ♛xd4 15 ♛h5+.

c) **13...♝a5** 14 bxc3 ♛xd4 15 ♛f7+ ♚d8 16 ♖d1 ♝xc3+ 17 ♚e2 wins Black's queen.

d) **13...♛xd4 14 ♛h5+ ♚d8 15 axb4 ♛e4+ 16 ♝e2 ♞xe2 17 ♛xe2 ♛h7 18 ♛d2+** *(68c)* and then:

d1) **18...♞d7** and **18...♝d7** are both met by 19 ♛xh6 – another knight-fork trick.

d2) **18...♚e8** 19 0-0 ♛xh8 20 ♖fd1 ♝d7 21 ♛d6 (threatening ♖xa7) 21...♚f7 (21...a6 22 ♛c7) 22 ♖a3 with a strong attack.

d3) **18...♚c7** 19 ♛d6+ ♚b7 20 ♖d1 ♛xh8 21 ♛e7+ ♝d7 (21...♚b6 22 f4) 22 f4 ♛e8 23 ♛g7 ♚c7 24 0-0 a5 25 f5 axb4 26 fxe6 ♛xe6 27 ♖d6 ♛e8 (27...♛g4 28 ♖xd7+) 28 ♖xh6 c3 29 bxc3 b3 30 e6 b2 31 c4 ♖a2 32 cxb5 cxb5 33 ♛e5+ 1-0 Stefansson-Inkiov, Gausdal International 1990.

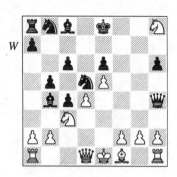

68a: after 11...♝b4

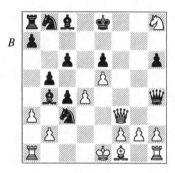

68b: after 13 ♛f3

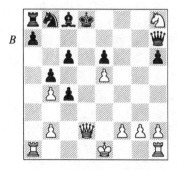

68c: after 18 ♛d2+

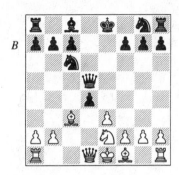

69a: after 8 ♘e2

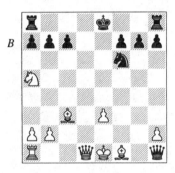

69b: after 13 ♘a5

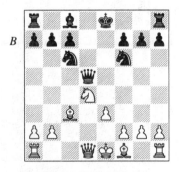

69c: after 9 ♘xd4

Surprise 69   W

Soundness: 3   Surprise Value: 3

Chigorin: Costa's idea

The Chigorin Queen's Gambit, **1 d4 d5 2 c4 ♘c6** has undergone a revival in recent years. A novel reply is **3 cxd5 ♕xd5 4 e3 e5 5 ♘c3 ♗b4 6 ♗d2 ♗xc3 7 ♗xc3 exd4 8 ♘e2** *(69a)*. If Black does nothing dramatic, White hopes that the bishop pair will give him the advantage.

a) **8...♘ge7** 9 ♘xd4 0-0 10 ♘xc6 ♕xc6 11 ♕d4 ♕g6 12 ♗d3 ♗f5 13 ♗xf5 ♘xf5 14 ♕f4 ♘d6 15 0-0 ± Nikolaidis-Miladinović, Aegina 1996.

b) **8...♗g4 9 f3** and then:

b1) **9...♗e6** 10 ♘xd4 ♘xd4 (10...0-0-0 11 ♕a4!) 11 ♕xd4 ♕xd4 12 ♗xd4 ±.

b2) **9...♖d8** 10 ♘xd4 ♘xd4?? 11 ♕xd4 wins material.

b3) **9...♗xf3** 10 gxf3 ♕xf3 is the attempt to do something dramatic, but White is better after 11 ♘xd4 ♕xh1 12 ♘xc6 ♘f6 (12...♕xh2 13 ♕g4 ♘f6 14 ♕xg7! favours White) 13 ♘a5! *(69b)* 13...♕xh2 (13...♘d5 14 ♕d4!) 14 ♕a4+ c6 15 0-0-0! 0-0 16 ♗xf6 gxf6 17 ♘xb7 ♖ab8 18 ♗a6 ♕e5 19 ♕a3! ± San Segundo-Gallego, Linares Open 1997.

c) **8...♘f6 9 ♘xd4** *(69c)*:

c1) **9...♘e4?** 10 ♘b5! ♕xd1+ 11 ♖xd1 0-0 12 ♘xc7 ♘xc3 13 bxc3 ♗g4 14 ♘xa8 ♗xd1 15 ♔xd1 ♖xa8 16 ♗e2 ♔f8 17 ♔c2 led to an endgame win for White in Costa-Baumhus, Gelsenkirchen 1991.

c2) **9...0-0** 10 ♘b5 ♕g5 11 h4 (11 ♘xc7, as played by Van Wely, is riskier) 11...♕g6 12 h5 ♕g5 13 h6 ♗g4 (Kachiani-Botsari, Pula wom Echt 1997) and now 14 ♕a4 looks strong.

Surprise 70   *B*

Soundness: 3   Surprise Value: 3

The Chandler Variation

In the main line of the QGD Tarrasch, **1 d4
d5 2 c4 e6 3 ♘c3 c5 4 cxd5 exd5 5 ♘f3 ♘c6
6 g3 ♘f6 7 ♗g2 ♗e7 8 0-0 0-0 9 ♗g5 cxd4
10 ♘xd4 h6 11 ♗e3 ♖e8 12 ♖c1**, Murray
Chandler has played the move **12...♗e6**
(70a) (instead of the traditional 12...♗f8
and 12...♗g4) many times, with excellent
results. This move solidly defends the d5-
pawn and wastes no time on possibly unnecessary prophylaxis. Black directly invites a
discussion of one of the key themes in the
Tarrasch: is it favourable for White to exchange on e6? Black hopes that in that case
his pawn centre (after ...fxe6) will prove
strong, and that if White doesn't take, then
kingside play following ...♕d7 and ...♗h3
will be effective.

   a) **13 ♘cb5** (?! – Gligorić) 13...♗d7! 14
♗f4 ♘xd4 15 ♘xd4 ♕b6 16 ♘b3 ♕a6 17
♗e5 ♗g4 18 f3 ♗e6 = Gligorić-A.Zaitsev,
Busum 1969.

   b) **13 ♘xe6** fxe6 14 ♗d2 (intending e4)
was Gligorić's recommendation, which has
not been tested at GM level.

   c) **13 ♘a4** ♕d7 14 ♘c5 (14 ♘xe6 fxe6
15 ♗c5 ♖ad8 16 ♕b3?! ♘a5 17 ♕b4 b6 18
♗xe7 ♕xe7 was absolutely OK for Black in
Burgess-Chandler, British League (4NCL)
1995/6) 14...♗xc5 15 ♖xc5 ♗h3 16 ♘xc6
bxc6 17 ♕a4 *(70b)* 17...♗xg2 18 ♔xg2 ♘g4
19 ♕xc6 ♕xc6 20 ♖xc6 ♘xe3+ 21 fxe3 ♖xe3
ought to be survivable for Black, Lodhi-
S.Brown, London Lloyds Bank 1994.

   d) **13 ♕b3** ♕d7 14 ♘xe6 fxe6 15 ♖fd1
♔h8 16 h3 ♗f8 17 f4 ♕f7 18 ♗f2 ♗b4 19

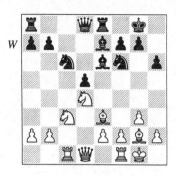

70a: after 12...♗e6

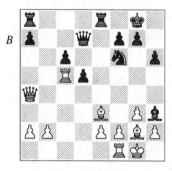

70b: after 17 ♕a4

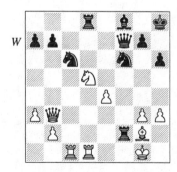

70c: after 24...♖xf2

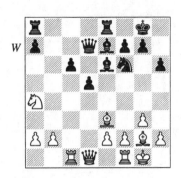

70d: after 14...♕d7

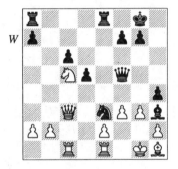

70e: after 22...h4

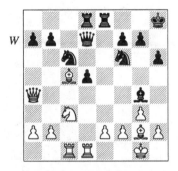

70f: after 17...♗g4

♘a4 ♗f8 20 a3 e5 21 fxe5 ♖xe5 22 ♘c3 ♖f5 23 ♘xd5 ♖d8 24 e4 (24 ♗c5!?) 24...♖xf2! *(70c)* 25 ♔xf2 ♘xe4++ 26 ♔g1 ♕f2+ 27 ♔h2 ♗d6 28 ♖c3 ♘a5 29 ♕c2 ♗xg3+ 30 ♔h1 ♕xc2 31 ♖xc2 ♘f2+ 32 ♖xf2 ♗xf2 and Black ought to be the one with the winning chances, Van Wely-Chandler, European Clubs Cup 1996.

e) **13 ♘xc6 bxc6 14 ♘a4 ♕d7** *(70d)* and then:

e1) **15 ♗c5** ♗h3 16 ♕d3 (16 ♗e7 ♗xg2 17 ♔xg2 ♖xe7 18 e3 ♘e4 = K.Norman-Giddins, British League (4NCL) 1996) 16...♗xg2 17 ♔xg2 ♕g4 18 ♗d4 ♖ac8 19 ♖c2 ♘h7 20 h3 ♕d7 21 f4 ♘f8 ∓ (the knight is heading for good squares one way or another) Wilson-Chandler, British League (4NCL) 1996.

e2) **15 ♘c5** ♗xc5 16 ♗xc5 ♗h3 17 ♗d4 ♗xg2 18 ♔xg2 ♘e4 ∓ Rodriguez – Shkurovich-Khasin, corr 1990.

e3) **15 ♖e1** ♗h3 16 ♗h1 ♘g4 17 ♗d4 ♗b4 18 ♗c3 ♕f5 19 f3 ♘e3 20 ♕d4 ♗xc3 21 ♕xc3 h5 22 ♘c5 h4 *(70e)* 23 ♘e4 (White is fortunate to have this) 23...♖xe4 24 fxe4 ♕g5 25 ♔f2 ♘g4+ 26 ♔g1 ♘e3 27 ♔f2 ♘g4+ 28 ♔g1 ♘e3 ½-½ Knaak-Chandler, Bundesliga 1996/7.

f) **13 ♕a4** ♕d7 14 ♖fd1 (14 ♘xe6 fxe6 15 ♖cd1 ♗f8 16 ♘e4 ♘xe4 17 ♗xe4 ♕f7 18 ♗b1, Spraggett-Gentes, Winnipeg 1997, 18...♘e5 should give Black kingside counterplay) 14...♔h8 15 ♘b3 ♖ad8 16 ♘c5 ♗xc5 17 ♗xc5 ♗g4 *(70f)* (setting up an interesting tactical interchange) 18 ♗xd5 ♗xe2 19 ♗xc6 ♗xd1 20 ♗xd7 ♖e1+ 21 ♔g2 ♗xa4 22 ♖xe1 ♗xd7 23 ♗xa7 ♗c6+ 24 ♔g1 ♖d2 25 ♖e2 ♖d3 26 ♖e3 ♖d2 27 ♖e2 ♖d3 28 ♗e3 ♘e4 29 ♘xe4 ♗xe4 30 ♖d2 ♖xd2 31 ♗xd2 ♗f3 and Black should hold, Sadler-Chandler, British League (4NCL) 1996/7.

Surprise 71   W

Soundness: 4   Surprise Value: 3

QGA: 7 e4!? pawn sacrifice

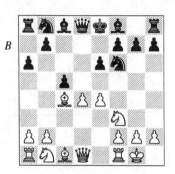

71a: after 7 e4

After **1 d4 d5 2 c4 dxc4 3 ♘f3 ♘f6 4 e3 e6 5 ♗xc4 c5 6 0-0 a6**, the pawn sacrifice **7 e4** *(71a)* is nothing new – it was played in the 1950s and 1960s by Petrosian, Geller and co. However, it was thought to promise little, and was more or less abandoned. A horrible loss by Kasparov in 1982 ensured another decade and a half of obscurity. It is only in the last year that the true power of 7 e4 has been recognized.

Here we consider two ways for Black to decline the pawn. In the next Surprise we see what happens to Black if he captures on e4.

a) **7...cxd4 8 e5 ♘fd7 9 ♕xd4 ♘c6 10 ♕f4!** and now:

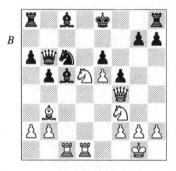

71b: after 19 ♘d5

a1) **10...♕c7 11 ♖e1 ♘dxe5 12 ♘xe5 ♘xe5 13 ♕xe5 ♕xc4 14 ♘c3** (threatening ♘d5) **14...f6 15 ♕h5+ g6 16 ♕f3 ♗e7 17 ♗h6 ♕h4 18 ♘d5 ♔f7** (18...exd5 19 ♗g7 ♖f8 20 ♖xe7+!) **19 ♖ac1 ♕h5 20 ♖c7 1-0** Legky-Alet, Metz 1994.

a2) **10...b5 11 ♗b3 ♗b7 12 ♘c3 ♘c5 13 ♖d1 ♕c7 14 ♗c2 f5 15 ♗e3 ♗e7 16 ♗xc5 ♗xc5 17 ♗b3 ♗c8 18 ♖ac1 ♕b6 19 ♘d5!** *(71b)* **19...exd5 20 ♗xd5 ♖b8 21 ♗xc6+ ♕xc6 22 e6 +−** Rustemov-Mirzoev, Koszalin 1997.

b) **7...b5 8 ♗d3** and then:

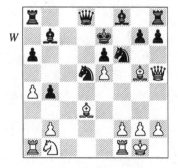

71c: after 15...♘7f6

b1) **8...cxd4 9 a4** (9 e5 ♘d5 10 ♘xd4 ±) I.Sokolov-Yakovich, Leeuwarden 1997) and now:

b11) **9...b4 10 e5 ♘d5 11 ♘xd4 ♗b7 12 ♕g4 ♘d7 13 ♘xe6** (and so begins the slaughter) **13...fxe6 14 ♕h5+ ♔e7 15 ♗g5+**

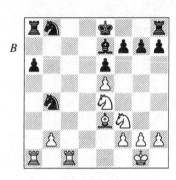

71d: after 18 ♘xe4

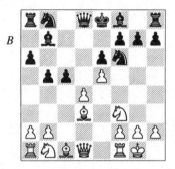

71e: after 9 e5

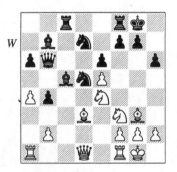

71f: after 16...0-0

♘7f6 *(71c)* 16 ♖e1 ♕e8 17 ♕f3 ♖d7 18 ♘d2 ♗f7 19 ♘e4 ♗e7 20 ♗c4 ♕d8 21 exf6 gxf6 22 ♕h5+ ♔g8 23 ♗h6 ♗f8 24 ♕g4+ ♔f7 25 ♘g5+ 1-0 Löffler-Jonkman, Wijk aan Zee 1996 – a highly entertaining game!

b12) **9...bxa4** 10 e5 ♘d5 11 ♕xa4+ ♗d7 12 ♕xd4 ♘b4 13 ♗e4 ♗c6 14 ♕xd8+ ♔xd8 15 ♘c3 ♗e7 16 ♗e3 ♔e8 17 ♖fc1 ♗xe4 18 ♘xe4 *(71d)* with a substantial plus for White due to Black's ramshackle queenside, Gelfand-Tkachev, Groningen FIDE Wch 1997.

b2) **8...♗b7 9 e5** *(71e)* (the new move, as opposed to Kasparov's limp 9 ♗g5) and then:

b21) **9...♘fd7** 10 ♘g5!? gives White a variety of crude but effective attacking ideas, e.g. 10...♘c6 11 d5!; 10...♕b6 11 ♕g4 cxd4 12 ♕f4; 10...cxd4 11 ♘xf7!; 10...♗e7 looks like Black's best try.

b22) **9...♘d5** and White even has a choice:

b221) **10 ♘bd2** ♘d7 (10...cxd4 11 a4 ♘b4 12 ♘e4 ♕d5 13 ♖e1 ♘xd3 14 ♕xd3 ♘c6 15 ♗f4 h6 looks unclear, B.Maksimović-Semkov, Iraklion 1993) 11 a4 ♕b6 12 axb5 axb5 13 ♖xa8+ ♗xa8 (Aleksandrov-Vaulin, Russia Cup (Krasnodar) 1997) 14 dxc5! ♘xc5 15 ♗b1 ±.

b222) **10 ♗g5** ♕b6 11 dxc5 ♗xc5 12 ♘c3 h6 13 ♗h4 ♘d7 (after 13...♘xc3 14 bxc3 0-0 White keeps an edge as long as he plays on both sides of the board: 15 a4 ♘d7 16 ♕e2 ±) 14 a4 b4?! (14...0-0!? 15 ♗g3! ±) 15 ♘e4 ♖c8 16 ♗g3 0-0 *(71f)* (Avrukh-Baburin, Groningen 1995) and now Avrukh indicated the line 17 ♕e2! ♗e7 18 ♘fd2 ♕d4 19 ♘b3 ♕b6 20 a5 ♕a7 21 ♔h1!? (intending ♖ae1 and f4 ±) 21...♘c5 22 ♘bxc5 ♗xc5 23 ♕g4 ♔h8 24 ♘g5!? with a kingside attack.

Surprise 72 W

Soundness: 4 Surprise Value: 3

QGA: 7 e4!? ♘xe4

After **1 d4 d5 2 c4 dxc4 3 ♘f3 ♘f6 4 e3 e6 5 ♗xc4 c5 6 0-0 a6 7 e4** Black most obvious move is to take the impudent pawn: **7...♘xe4** *(72a)*.

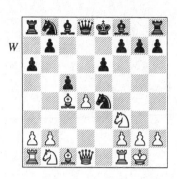

72a: after 7...♘xe4

However, the open e-file and White's development advantage then promise Black a difficult ride. White has two interesting and promising ways to continue. The former is less well proven, but leads to some beautiful variations. The critical line seems to depend on a position where White has powerful play for two pawns, as envisaged by Avrukh. The latter generally sees White either winning back the sacrificed pawn at the cost of some simplification, or keeping Black under the cosh in a complex middlegame.

a) **8 ♕e2!? ♘f6** (8...♘d6 9 dxc5 ±) **9 d5** and now:

a1) **9...b5** looks inadequate: 10 dxe6 bxc4 (10...fxe6 11 ♗xe6 ♕e7 12 ♘g5 ♗xe6 13 ♘xe6 was clearly better for White in Halkias-Fanouraki, Aegina 1996) 11 ♖d1 ♕b6 12 exf7+ ♔xf7 13 ♘g5+ ♔g6 14 ♖d5!! *(72b)*

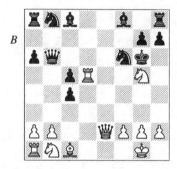

72b: after 14 ♖d5

14...♘xd5 15 ♕e8+ ♔f5 16 g4+ ♔xg4 17 ♕xc8+ ♔h5 18 ♕e8+ g6 (18...♕g6 19 ♕e2+ ♔h4 20 ♕xc4+ ♔h5 21 ♕e2+ ♔h4 22 ♕f3) 19 ♕e2+ ♔h6 20 ♕e5 1-0 Trofimov-Metliakhin, Russian Cht (Moscow) 1994. An astonishing sequence.

a2) **9...♘xd5** 10 ♖d1 ♕e7! (10...♗e7 11 ♘c3 0-0 12 ♗xd5 exd5 13 ♘xd5 puts Black under great pressure) 11 ♗g5 f6 12 ♗xd5 exd5 13 ♕d2 ♗e6 14 ♖e1 ♘c6 15 ♘c3 0-0-0 16 ♗f4! *(72c)* intending ♘a4 (Avrukh, Tyomkin) gives White dangerous play.

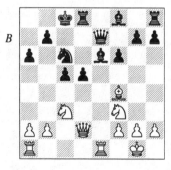

72c: after 16 ♗f4

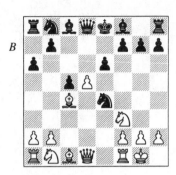

72d: after 8 d5

72e: after 12 ♗f4

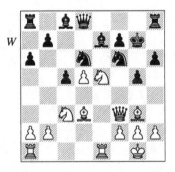

72f: after 16...♔g7

b) **8 d5!?** *(72d)* is the more reliable move:

b1) **8...b5** 9 dxe6 bxc4 (9...♕xd1 10 exf7+ ♔e7 11 ♖xd1 bxc4 12 ♖e1) 10 exf7+ ♔e7 11 ♕e1 regains the piece with a substantial advantage.

b2) **8...exd5** 9 ♗xd5 ♘d6 10 ♖e1+ ♗e7 11 ♗g5 f6 12 ♗f4 ± Chekhov.

b3) **8...♘d6** 9 dxe6 ♗xe6 (9...fxe6 10 ♗d3 ♗e7 11 ♕c2 ♘f5 12 ♖d1 with excellent compensation) 10 ♗xe6 fxe6 11 ♖e1 and Black is in some trouble.

b4) **8...♘f6** 9 ♖e1! ♗e7 10 dxe6 ♗xe6 11 ♕xd8+ ♗xd8 (11...♔xd8 12 ♗xe6 fxe6 13 ♘g5 ♔c8 14 ♘xe6 g6 15 ♗g5 ♘bd7 16 ♘c3 ±) 12 ♗xe6 (12 ♘g5!?) 12...fxe6 13 ♘g5 (Black survived after 13 ♖xe6+ ♗e7 14 ♘c3 ♘c6 15 ♗f4 0-0 in Aleksandrov-Sadler, Køge 1997 – a game that reached this position via 8...♗e7) and now 13...0-0 14 ♘xe6 ♖e8 15 ♘c3 b6 16 ♗g5 ♘c6 17 ♘a4 +– is a line cited by Tsesarsky.

b5) **8...♗e7** 9 ♖e1 exd5 (9...♘f6 transposes to 'b4') 10 ♕xd5 ♘d6 11 ♗d3 0-0 12 ♗f4 *(72e)* 12...♘f5 13 ♘c3 ♗f6 14 ♗xf5 ♕xd5 15 ♗xh7+ ♔xh7 16 ♘xd5 ± Gelfand-Lautier, Belgrade 1997.

b6) **8...e5** 9 ♖e1 ♘d6 10 ♘xe5 ♗e7 11 ♗d3 h6 (11...0-0 12 ♕c2) 12 ♕h5 ♔f8 (12...0-0 13 ♘c3 ♘d7 14 ♗xh6 gxh6 15 ♕xh6 +–) 13 ♘c3 ♘d7 14 ♗f4 ♘f6 15 ♕f3 g5 16 ♗g3 ♔g7 *(72f)* 17 ♖e3 h5 18 h3 g4 19 ♕f4 ♘fe8 20 ♘e4 h4 21 ♗h2 gxh3 22 gxh3 ♘f5 23 ♔h1! ♔f8 24 ♖g1 with a winning attack, Rustemov-Kharlov, Russian Ch (Elista) 1996

Surprise 73　**W**

Soundness: 5　Surprise Value: 3

Old Indian 4...♗f5 5 ♘g5!

The idea of playing, after **1 ♘f3 d6 2 d4 ♘f6 3 c4 g6 4 ♘c3**, the move **4...♗f5**, to cause White some inconvenience if he wishes to play e4, was developed in the 1980s by a group of Americans, notably Joel Benjamin. One of the key ideas is that after 5 ♘h4 ♗d7, White will shortly need to drop his knight back to f3. Then the position will be like a normal King's Indian, except that Black has managed to play the move ...♗d7 (which is probably of some use) entirely for free.

The move played by White in the short game Gausel-Hodgson, Oslo 1994, which follows, is considered by the American analysts to be virtually a refutation of the idea.

5 ♘g5! *(73a)* **5...♗g7?!** (instead after 5...h6 6 e4, 6...hxg5 7 exf5 gxf5 8 ♗xg5 ♘e4 9 ♘xe4 fxe4 10 ♕c2 is good for White, while 6...♗g4 7 ♘f3 is a version of King's Indian where ...♗g4 is not too good, and ...h6 could well be worse than useless) **6 e4 ♗g4 7 f3! ♗c8** (7...♗d7 would here be unfortunate due to 8 e5!) **8 f4** *(73b)*. This is a King's Indian, Four Pawns Attack, except that White's knight is on g5 rather than g1. **8...0-0** (8...h6 9 ♘f3 is a Four Pawns, with Black having spent a tempo on ...h6) **9 ♗e2 e5?** (9...c5) **10 dxe5 dxe5 11 ♕xd8 ♖xd8 12 fxe5 ♘e8** (12...♘g4 13 e6; 12...♘fd7 13 e6) **13 0-0** *(73c)* **1-0** (13...♗e6 14 ♘xe6 fxe6 15 ♗g5; 13...♗xe5 14 ♘xf7 ♗d4+ 15 ♔h1 ♖d7 16 ♘h6+ ♔g7 17 ♗g4; 13...f6 14 exf6 ♘xf6 15 c5 and ♗c4+).

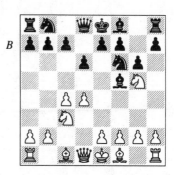

73a: after 5 ♘g5

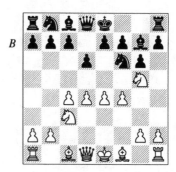

73b: after 8 f4

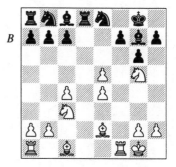

73c: after 13 0-0

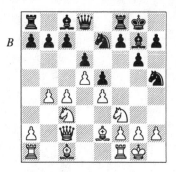

74a: after 10 ♕c2

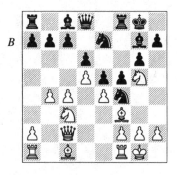

74b: after 12 ♗f3

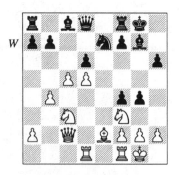

74c: after 15...cxd6

Surprise 74   W

Soundness: 3   Surprise Value: 5

KID: Epishin's 10 ♕c2

In mid-1995, in the position after **1 d4 ♘f6 2 c4 g6 3 ♘c3 ♗g7 4 e4 d6 5 ♘f3 0-0 6 ♗e2 e5 7 0-0 ♘c6 8 d5 ♘e7 9 b4 ♘h5** the world (or at least the King's Indian-playing world) was stunned by Ivan Sokolov's novelty **10 ♖e1**. At the very end of 1997 came another completely new move in this position: Epishin's **10 ♕c2** (74a). Will this be 'the new ♖e1' and blossom into a full system with its own sophisticated themes?

One motivation may be that after 10 c5 ♘f4 11 ♗xf4 exf4, White would like to play 12 ♕c2, but his position is then a bit too loose, with 12...f5 possible. Instead in that line 12 ♕d2 h6 13 ♖ad1 g5 14 e5 g4 seems satisfactory for Black – with the queen on c2 and the d1-rook opposing the black queen directly, things are a little different. Here are some lines:

a) **10...a5** 11 bxa5 (11 ♗a3?! axb4 12 ♗xb4 c5 13 dxc6 ♘xc6) and Black has the normal choice: 11...c5 or 11...♖xa5.

b) **10...f5** 11 ♘g5 ♘f4 12 ♗f3!? (74b), e.g. 12...h6?! 13 ♗xf4 exf4 (13...fxe4 14 ♗xe4) 14 ♘e6 ♗xe6 15 dxe6.

c) **10...♘f4 11 ♗xf4 exf4 12 ♖ad1**:

c1) **12...h6** (intending ...g5) 13 c5 g5 (13...f5?! 14 e5 dxe5 15 d6) 14 e5 g4 15 exd6 cxd6 (74c) 16 ♘d4 (16 ♘d2 dxc5) 16...dxc5 17 bxc5 ♘xd5 18 ♘db5 looks good for White.

c2) **12...♗g4** 13 ♘d4 ♗xe2 14 ♘cxe2 a5 15 b5 ♗e5 16 ♘f3 ♘c8 17 c5 ♕e7 18 ♘xe5 ♕xe5 19 f3 ♖e8 20 ♘c1 ♕f6 21 ♘d3 g5 22 ♖c1 ± Epishin-Brustman, Aschach 1997.

Surprise 75   *W*

Soundness: 4   Surprise Value: 3

KI Four Pawns: 6...♘a6 7 e5

In the Four Pawns Attack, **1 d4 ♘f6 2 c4 g6 3 ♘c3 ♗g7 4 e4 d6 5 f4 0-0 6 ♘f3**, Black's most popular line is **6...♘a6**. I recommend that White investigate **7 e5**, meeting **7...♘d7** with the calm **8 ♗e2**, rather than any berserk attacking attempt. After **8...c5 9 exd6** *(75a)* Black has a choice:

a) **9...exd6 10 0-0!?** (10 d5 is interesting too) 10...♖e8 11 f5!? *(75b)* 11...cxd4 12 ♘d5 ♘c7 13 fxg6 hxg6 14 ♗g5 ♘f6 15 ♘xf6+ ♗xf6 16 ♗xf6 ♕xf6 17 ♘xd4 ♕g5 18 ♗f3 ♘e6 19 ♗d5 gave White an attractive position in Rausis-McShane, Hastings 1997/8.

b) **9...cxd4 10 ♘xd4 ♘b6!? 11 0-0 ♕xd6 12 ♗e3 ♕c5** (12...♖d8 13 ♘db5 ♕xd1 14 ♖axd1 ♖xd1 15 ♖xd1 ♗e6 16 b3 is good for White; 12...♕b4 is dubious; 12...♗e6!? 13 b3 ♖fd8 14 ♘cb5 ♕b8 could be Black's best chance) **13 ♘e4 ♕c7 14 ♕b3 ♖d8 15 ♖ad1! ♗d7 16 c5** and here:

b1) **16...♘d5?!** 17 ♕xd5 ♗c6 18 ♕c4 ♗xe4 and now 19 ♘e6 was enough for an advantage in Vokač-Kovaliov, Ostrava 1993, but 19 ♘b5 ♕c6 20 ♘xa7! is better still.

b2) **16...♘xc5** 17 ♘xc5 ♕xc5 18 ♘b5 ♕f5 19 ♘xa7 ♘c8 has been recommended as fine for Black, with Gallagher citing **20 ♘xc8 ♖axc8 21 ♗b6 ♗e6 22 ♖xd8+ ♖xd8 23 ♕a3 ♖d2!**. However, **20 ♘b5!** *(75c)* looks good. Consider: the c8-knight has no good moves; the d7-bishop is pinned against an undefended rook; the black queen is a target; all the white pieces are well-placed.

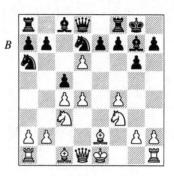

75a: after 9 exd6

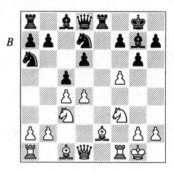

75b: after 11 f5

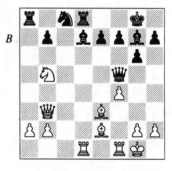

75c: after 20 ♘b5

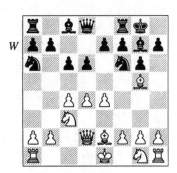

76a: after 7...c6

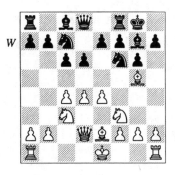

76b: after 8...♘c7

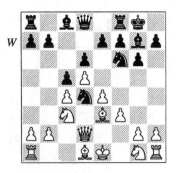

76c: after 11...♘d4

Surprise 76   B

Soundness: 3   Surprise Value: 3

Averbakh King's Indian

1 d4 ♘f6 2 c4 g6 3 ♘c3 ♗g7 4 e4 d6 5 ♗e2 0-0 6 ♗g5 ♘a6 7 ♕d2 c6 *(76a).*

With 7...c6 Black deviates from the normal move 7...e5. The idea is to continue with ...♘c7-e6, hitting the g5-bishop and putting pressure on the d4-pawn. This idea is well-known after 7 f4, but is much more unusual after the more common 7 ♕d2. However, it looks viable. White can reply:

a) **8 h4** ♘c7 9 h5 ♘e6 10 ♗e3 c5 11 d5 ♘d4 ∓ 12 ♗d1 e6 13 ♗h6 e5 14 ♘h3 ♗g4 15 ♗xg7 ♔xg7 16 ♗xg4 ♘xg4 17 f3? ♘e3! –+ Gaprindashvili-Baczinski, Baden-Baden 1991.

b) **8 ♘f3 ♘c7** *(76b)* and then:

b1) **9 d5** cxd5 10 cxd5 b5, for example 11 ♗xf6 ♗xf6 12 ♘xb5 ♘xb5 13 ♗xb5 ♖b8.

b2) **9 0-0** is best met by 9...♗g4 planning ...♘e6, possibly ...♗xf3 and ...c5. Instead 9...♘e6 puts d4 under less pressure.

b3) **9 e5** dxe5 10 dxe5 ♕xd2+ (10...♘d7 is more ambitious) 11 ♘xd2 ♘d7 12 ♗xe7 ♖e8 13 ♗d6 (S.Ivanov-Malishauskas, Katowice 1993) 13...♘e6 followed by ...♘f4 and ...♘xe5 is absolutely fine for Black.

c) **8 f3** (the 'main line', and probably best) **8...♘c7** and now:

c1) **9 ♗d1 ♘e6 10 ♗e3** (10 ♘ge2? was played against me by a player who is normally very solid and sensible; it shows the effect of the opening surprise: White 'forgets' that his bishop is attacked!) **10...c5** (10...♕a5) **11 d5** (11 ♘ge2 ♕b6) **11...♘d4** *(76c)* seems OK for Black:

c11) **12 ♗xd4** cxd4 gives Black excellent compensation following 13 ♕xd4, while 13 ♘b5 e5 14 dxe6 fxe6 15 ♘xd4? ♘xe4 is a fiasco for White.

c12) **12 ♘ge2** e5 13 dxe6 ♗xe6 14 ♘xd4 cxd4 15 ♗xd4 ♗xc4.

c2) **9 d5** *(76d)* is a logical move, preventing ...♘e6. Then 9...e6? 10 dxc6 bxc6 11 c5 is no good at all, while 9...cxd5 10 cxd5 e6 11 dxe6 ♘xe6 12 ♗e3 is unconvincing, so Black should play on the queenside, with 9...a6, 9...♖b8, 9...♗d7, or maybe 9...c5.

c3) **9 h4** gives Black a choice:

c31) **9...♘h5** 10 g4 ♘g3 11 ♖h3 ♘xe2 12 ♘gxe2 h5 13 ♖g3 hxg4 14 fxg4 (Zucchelli-Burgess, Gausdal Eikrem mem 1997) 14...b5 is quite good for Black since it is difficult for White to organize his kingside play.

c32) **9...♘e6** 10 ♗e3 (10 g4 ♘xg5 11 hxg5 ♘d7 and the idea of shifting the e2-bishop and playing ♕h2 is too slow since Black has time for ...♖e8 and ...♘f8) 10...c5 11 d5 ♘d4 12 ♗xd4 cxd4 13 ♕xd4 ♘h5 *(76e)* gives Black very good play for the pawn, e.g. 14 ♕f2? ♗e5; 14 ♕d2 ♘g3 15 ♖h2 ♕b6 (or 15...♗e5 16 f4 ♗xc3) 16 0-0-0 ♗e5 17 f4 ♗xc3 18 ♕xc3 ♘xe4; 14 ♕e3 ♘g3 15 ♖h2 f5 leads to a very difficult position for White. Black has various active ideas, while White's freeing attempt 16 f4 can be met by 16...♘xe4 or 16...♗xc3+ and 17...♘xe4.

c4) **9 g4** ♘e6 10 ♗e3 c5 11 d5 ♘d4 *(76f)* 12 ♘b5 ♘xb5 (12...♗xg4!? leads to interesting tactics, but is totally unnecessary given how good Black's position is after normal play) 13 cxb5 a6 14 bxa6 b6 15 ♗b5 ♗xa6 16 ♗xa6 ♖xa6 17 ♘e2 ♕a8 18 ♘c3 b5 19 ♘xb5 ♖xa2 20 ♖xa2 ♕xa2 ∓ Mortazavi-Burgess, London tt 1997.

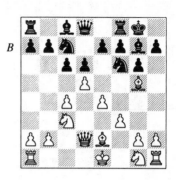

76d: after 9 d5

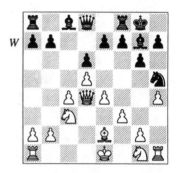

76e: after 13...♘h5

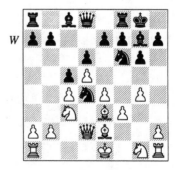

76f: after 11...♘d4

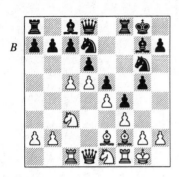

77a: after 14 c5

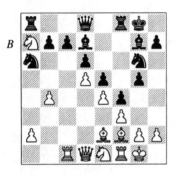

77b: after 17 ♘xa7

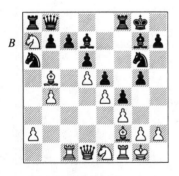

77c: after 18 ♗b5

Surprise 77   W

Soundness: 3   Surprise Value: 2

King's Indian: Kožul Gambit

After **1 d4 ♘f6 2 c4 g6 3 ♘c3 ♗g7 4 e4 d6 5 ♗e2 0-0 6 ♘f3 e5 7 0-0 ♘c6 8 d5 ♘e7 9 ♘e1 ♘d7 10 ♗e3 f5 11 f3 f4 12 ♗f2 g5**, the rook move **13 ♖c1** used to be just one of several ways to prepare a standard pawn-push on the queenside. Then after **13...♘g6** Kožul unleashed his pawn-sacrifice idea **14 c5** *(77a)* in place of 14 b4 ♘f6 15 c5 ♖f7, which has been regarded as too slow for White ever since the game Piket-Kasparov, Tilburg 1989. Since 14...dxc5 15 b4! is very good for White after either 15...cxb4 16 ♘b5 or 15...b6 16 ♘d3, Black replies **14...♘xc5 15 b4 ♘a6** (c7 caves in after 15...♘d7? 16 ♘b5). White intends that the sidelined knight on a6 will hamstring Black attacking attempts (only one knight to sacrifice on the kingside...) and prove a target for White's queenside play too. **16 ♘b5** (16 ♘d3 h5 17 ♘b5 ♗d7 18 a4 ♗h6 19 ♖c3 b6 20 ♗e1 ♖f7 21 ♘f2 ♘h4 22 ♘xd6 cxd6 23 ♗xa6 ♕e8 24 ♕e2 g4 ½-½ Piket-Kasparov, Linares 1997) **16...♗d7** (16...♖f7 17 ♕a4 intends ♕a5, while 16...b6 can be met by 17 ♕a4 planning to win back the pawn and open lines by ♘xd6 and ♗xa6) **17 ♘xa7!** *(77b)* (the latest refinement; 17 ♕a4 g4 18 fxg4 f3 19 gxf3 ♘f4 20 ♕d1 h5! gave Black good counterplay in the stem game, Kožul-Fedorowicz, Wijk aan Zee 1991) and now Black has a wide choice:

a) **17...♘xb4?** 18 ♕b3 is very good for White after both 18...♘a6 19 ♕xb7 and 18...♕b8 19 ♕xb4 ♖xa7 20 ♗xa7 ♕xa7+ 21 ♔h1.

b) **17...g4?!** (premature; compare line 'e2') 18 fxg4 f3 19 ♘xf3 (19 gxf3!? and 19 ♗xa6 are both greedy, but there's no obvious punishment) 19...♗xg4 (19...♘f4? 20 ♗xa6 bxa6 21 ♘c6 ♕e8 22 h3 +−) 20 ♗xa6 bxa6 21 ♘c6 ♕e8 22 ♗g3 ±.

c) **17...♕b8** (the reason why 17 ♘xa7 was initially rejected by Kožul in 1991, but White turns out to have a good reply) 18 ♗b5! *(77c)* gives White a definite advantage after either 18...♖d8 19 ♗xd7 ♖xd7 20 ♕a4 ♖f7 21 ♘b5 or 18...♗xb5 19 ♘xb5 ♘xb4 20 ♖xc7 ♖a5 21 a4 ♖xb5 22 ♖xg7+ ♔xg7 23 axb5.

d) **17...♖f7** (this looks sensible) 18 ♕c2 ♕f6 19 ♗xa6 bxa6 (D.Gurevich-Leitao, Groningen 1997) and now 20 ♕e2!? *(77d)* must be the way to proceed.

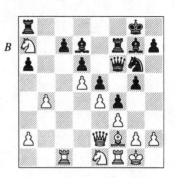

77d: after 20 ♕e2

e) **17...h5** and now:

e1) **18 a4 ♗h6 19 ♖c4 ♖f7 20 ♘b5 ♖g7 21 ♔h1 ♘f8 22 g3 fxg3 23 ♗xg3 ♘g6 24 ♘d3** *(77e)* has occurred in two games:

e11) **24...♘f4** 25 ♗xf4 gxf4 26 ♖g1 ♖xg1+ 27 ♕xg1+ ♔h7 28 ♗f1 ♕e7 29 ♘xc7 ♖c8 30 ♕b6 ♗xa4 (Atalik-Gufeld, Waikiki 1997) 31 ♕xb7 ♖xc7 32 ♕xa6 wins a pawn.

e12) **24...♔h7** 25 ♖g1 ♖f7 26 ♗f2 ♗e8 27 ♘c3 ♘b8 28 ♕c2 c6 *(77f)* is a typical and messy position. Maybe White should try to smash open some lines on the queenside by **29 dxc6** bxc6 30 b5, as after **29 a5** ♕f6 30 ♘a4 (Yermolinsky-Kindermann, Groningen FIDE Wch rpd 1997) Black could have played the trick 30...b5! (31 axb6 cxd5).

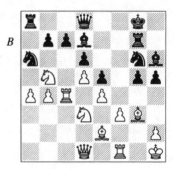

77e: after 24 ♘d3

e2) **18 a3** g4? (18...♖f7 leads to more normal play, with White probably needing to throw in a well-timed ♗xa6 if he is to get anywhere) 19 fxg4 f3 20 ♗xf3 hxg4 21 ♗xg4 ♖xf2 22 ♖xf2 ♖xa7 23 ♖c3 ♖a8 24 ♖g3 ♘f4 25 ♘c2 ♕e7 26 ♘e3 ♖f8 27 ♗xd7 ♕xd7 28 ♖g5 and White, rather unusually for this variation, won by an attack on the kingside in Korchnoi-M.Ivanov, Enghien les Bains 1997.

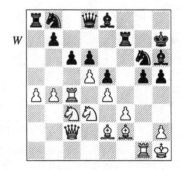

77f: after 28...c6

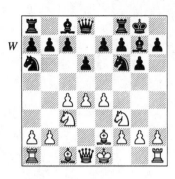

78a: after 6...♞a6

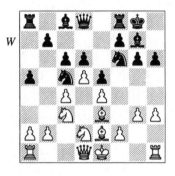

78b: after 15...a5

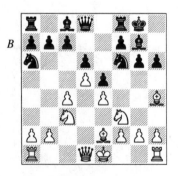

78c: after 9 d5

Surprise 78   *B*

Soundness: 3   Surprise Value: 3

KID: Kazakh Variation

In the position after **1 d4 ♞f6 2 c4 g6 3 ♞c3 ♝g7 4 e4 d6 5 ♞f3 0-0 6 ♝e2**, as soon as it became clear that 6...e5 7 0-0 ♞a6 was a playable system for Black, some players started to wonder whether **6...♞a6** *(78a)* might be worth trying, possibly following up with ...e5, or possibly striking out on some different course. If nothing else, it causes move-order problems to those wishing to play the Gligorić (6...e5 7 ♝e3) or the Petrosian System (6...e5 7 d5), and it certainly winds up those boring Exchange Variation players.

a) **7 e5** dxe5 8 ♞xe5 c5 9 ♝e3 cxd4 10 ♝xd4 ♞d7 11 ♞xd7 ♛xd7 12 ♝xg7 ♛xd1+ 13 ♜xd1 ♚xg7 is OK for Black, Bruk-Tsifanskaya, Israeli League 1997.

b) **7 ♝e3** is normally met by 7...e5, but Black can safely hit the bishop by 7...♞g4, or experiment with 7...♛e8.

c) **7 ♝f4** ♞h5 8 ♝g5 h6 9 ♝e3 e5 10 g3 ♞f6 11 d5 ♞g4 12 ♝d2 c6 13 h3 ♞f6 14 ♝e3 ♞c5 15 ♞d2 a5 *(78b)* and by comparison with a line of the Petrosian System, Black has gained the useful move ...c6, and White the moves g3 and h3, which are less clearly beneficial, Zviagintsev-Tkachev, Biel 1995.

d) **7 ♝g5** actually transposes to a minor variation of the Averbakh, but is White's best attempt to reach a Petrosian System. Black can acquiesce, by 7...h6 8 ♝h4 e5 9 d5 *(78c)*, content that this reaches the line 6...e5 7 d5 ♞a6 8 ♝g5 h6 9 ♝h4, having circumvented 8 ♞d2, which is White's most dangerous try in that line.

Surprise 79 *B*

Soundness: 2   Surprise Value: 4

Grünfeld: 5 ♗g5 c5

After **1 d4 ♘f6 2 c4 g6 3 ♘c3 d5 4 ♗g5 ♗g7 5 ♘f3**, the move **5...c5!?** *(79a)* will certainly surprise most players. I can't say I trust it too much, but judge for yourself:

a) **6 dxc5 ♕a5 7 cxd5** and then:

a1) **7...♘e4?** 8 ♗d2 ♘xd2 (8...♘xc3 9 bxc3 ♗xc3 10 ♖c1) 9 ♕xd2 ♘a6 10 e3 ♘xc5 11 ♗b5+ ♗d7 12 ♗xd7+ has given Zilberman two convincing victories as White.

a2) **7...♘xd5** 8 ♕xd5 ♗xc3+ 9 ♗d2 is a position more commonly reached via 4 ♗f4 ♗g7 5 ♘f3 c5, etc. Then **9...♗xd2+** 10 ♕xd2 ♕xc5 11 ♖c1 ♕f5 12 ♘d4 ♕d7 is dubious in view of 13 ♕h6! *(79b)*, while **9...♗e6!** 10 ♕xb7 ♗xd2+ 11 ♘xd2 0-0 12 b4 ♕a4 13 e3! keeps an edge, Van Wely-Kamsky, Groningen 1995.

b) **6 ♗xf6 ♗xf6 7 cxd5** (the insipid 7 ♘xd5?! ♗g7 8 e3 ♘c6 gave Black at least comfortable equality in Cifuentes-I.Sokolov, Dutch Ch (Amsterdam) 1996) **7...♕b6** *(79c)* and then:

b1) **8 e4** cxd4 9 ♘b5 ♗g4 10 ♖c1 ♘a6 11 ♘bxd4 ♗xf3 12 ♘xf3 ♗xb2 13 ♖c2 is probably tenable for Black, Burgess-Skjelde, Gausdal International 1990.

b2) **8 ♖c1** 0-0 9 dxc5 ♕xb2 10 ♕d2 ♕b4 11 e3 ♖d8 with decent play for Black, Barsov-Cools, Vlissingen 1996.

b3) **8 e3** ♕xb2 9 ♘c1 ♕xc1+ 10 ♖xc1 cxd4 11 ♘b5 (11 ♗b5+?! ♔d8!) 11...♘a6 12 ♘bxd4 (Zviagintsev-Svidler, Yugoslav Cht (Tivat) 1995) and now Gagarin analysed 12...♘b4!? 13 ♗b5+ (13 ♗c4 ♗g4) 13...♔f8! as unclear.

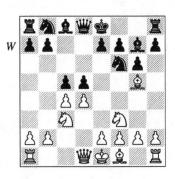

79a: after 5...c5

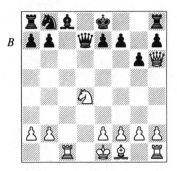

79b: after 13 ♕h6

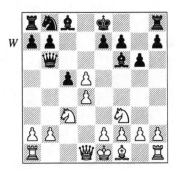

79c: after 7...♕b6

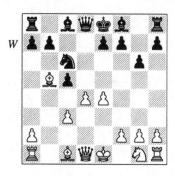

80a: after 7...♘c6

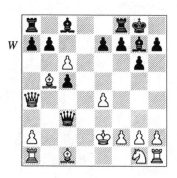

80b: after 11...0-0

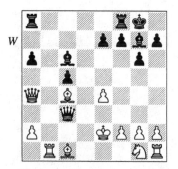

80c: after 14...♗c6

Surprise 80   *B*

Soundness: 3   Surprise Value: 2

Exchange Grünfeld: 6...c5

Following the moves **1 d4 ♘f6 2 c4 g6 3 ♘c3 d5 4 cxd5 ♘xd5 5 e4 ♘xc3 6 bxc3**, you might get the impression from some sources that **6...c5** (avoiding the popular modern line 6...♗g7 7 ♗b5+ c6 8 ♗a4) **7 ♗b5+** forces the less than dynamic 7...♗d7, when Black can only hope for equality. However, **7...♘c6!?** *(80a)* is playable, since following **8 d5 ♕a5!** (and not 8...a6?! 9 ♗e2! ♘a5 10 ♗e3, which gave White a useful advantage in I.Sokolov-H.Olafsson, Novi Sad OL 1990) **9 ♕a4 ♕xc3+ 10 ♔e2**, Black does not have to go in for 10...♗d7?, which loses after 11 dxc6 bxc6 12 ♗xc6 ♖d8 13 ♕b3!! ♕xa1 14 ♗b2 ♕b1 15 ♘f3! ♕xh1 16 ♘e5, as played, famously, in a simultaneous by Nezhmetdinov, and, many years later, in Yusupov-Morenz, Graz 1981. Instead, there is **10...♗g7! 11 dxc6 0-0** *(80b)*:

a) **12 cxb7?!** ♗xb7 13 ♖b1 c4! 14 ♗xc4 (14 ♕xc4 ♕xc4+ 15 ♗xc4 ♗xe4 16 ♖b3 ♗xg2 is a very nice tactical point) 14...♖ac8 15 ♗b5?! (but 15 ♗d5!? ♗a6+ 16 ♕xa6 ♕c2+ 17 ♗d2 ♕xb1 leaves Black with a powerful initiative) 15...a6! 16 ♗d2 axb5 17 ♕xb5 ♕c2 18 ♕xb7 ♖fd8 19 ♘f3 ♕d3+ 20 ♔d1 ♖c2 0-1 Kiselev-Dvoirys, Russian Ch (Elista) 1994.

b) **12 ♖b1** a6 13 cxb7 ♗xb7 14 ♗c4 ♗c6! *(80c)* 15 ♕b3 ♗xe4 16 ♕xc3 ♗xc3 17 ♖b3 ♗xg2 18 ♖xc3 ♗xh1 19 f3 ♖fd8 20 ♗e3 ♖ab8 is analysis by Arkhipov. He claims an edge for White, but Black's game looks wholly playable.

Surprise 81   W

Soundness: 2   Surprise Value: 4

Grünfeld: 5 ♗g5 and 8 ♕a4+

Here is an unusual idea for White: after **1 d4 ♘f6 2 ♘f3 g6 3 c4 ♗g7 4 ♘c3 d5 5 ♗g5 ♘e4 6 cxd5 ♘xg5 7 ♘xg5 e6**, instead of the normal (and not especially promising) moves 8 ♘f3 or 8 ♕d2, to play **8 ♕a4+** *(81a)*. A psychological factor comes into play: by playing 7...e6 rather than the speculative gambit 7...c6 Black has opted for a solid line. Black's soundest reply to the queen check is actually to play the ...c6 pawn-sacrifice idea – so at club level it is unlikely that Black will want to go in for this. The lines are as follows:

a) **8...♔f8?** 9 ♕b4+ ♔g8? 10 dxe6 ♕xg5 11 e7! ♗d7 12 ♕xb7 is the sort of trap Black might fall into.

b) **8...c6** 9 dxc6 ♘xc6 10 ♘f3 ♗d7 11 ♕d1!? (11 ♕a3 can be tried) 11...♕b6 12 ♕d2 *(81b)* 12...♘xd4! 13 0-0-0 ♖d8! 14 ♘xd4 ♗c6 15 e3 e5 16 ♕e1 exd4 17 exd4+ ♔f8 18 d5 ♗xd5 19 ♖xd5 ♖xd5 20 ♕e7+ ½-½ Shirov-Østenstad, Gausdal Troll 1991. Brilliant defence by Black – will your opponents manage as well?

c) **8...♗d7** 9 ♕b3 *(81c)* 9...♕xg5! (alternatively 9...exd5 10 ♕xd5 is an extra pawn) 10 ♕xb7 0-0 will give Black just enough if he plays very precisely. 11 ♕xa8 (kicking the black queen with 11 h4 is interesting) 11...♘c6 (11...♗xd4!? 12 e3 ♕e5 13 ♖c1 exd5 14 ♕b7 and now 14...♘c6 is essential) 12 h4 ♕g4 (12...♕h6 13 ♕b7 ♘xd4 14 ♔d1) 13 ♕b7 ♖b8 (13...♘xd4 14 ♖c1) 14 dxc6 1-0 Knaak-Siroky, Olomouc 1972.

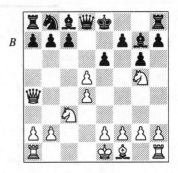

81a: after 8 ♕a4+

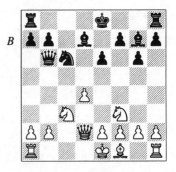

81b: after 12 ♕d2

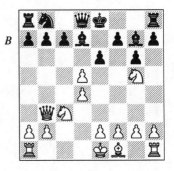

81c: after 9 ♕b3

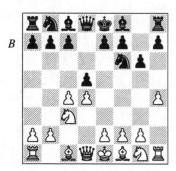

82a: after 4 h4

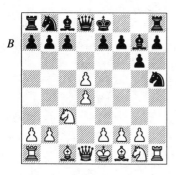

82b: after 6 cxd5

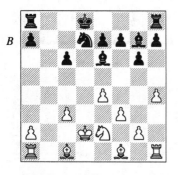

82c: after 13 ♘e2

Surprise 82   **W**

Soundness: 2   Surprise Value: 5

Grünfeld: Bayonet Attacks

After **1 d4 ♘f6 2 c4 g6 3 ♘c3 d5**, the weird move 4 g4 is quite well known, but **4 h4** *(82a)* is far rarer. Normally when seeing a move such as this, one would sceptically wonder what would happen if it were played against someone really strong. Well, is Smyslov strong enough?!

a) **4...♗g7 5 h5 ♘xh5** (5...0-0 6 hxg6 hxg6 7 cxd5 ♘xd5 8 e4 ♘xc3 9 bxc3 c5 is treacherous for Black: an Exchange Grünfeld where White has opened the h-file, albeit at the cost of two tempi; though White can't force a trivial mate, I think 10 ♗h6 looks best) **6 cxd5** *(82b)* and then:

a1) **6...c5** 7 dxc5 ♕a5 8 e4 (or 8 ♕a4+) 8...♕xc5 9 ♗e2 ♗d4 10 ♗xh5 ♗xf2+ 11 ♔f1 ♗xg1 12 ♖xg1 gxh5 13 ♕xh5 ♘d7 14 ♕e2 b6 15 ♗e3 ♕a5 16 ♘b5 ± Sulyok-A.Nemeth, Hungary tt 1994.

a2) **6...c6** 7 e4 cxd5 (Kadas-Gross, Tapolca 1986) and now 8 ♘xd5 is answered by 8...e6, but 8 e5!? is interesting, threatening g4. If Black wants to save his knight he must play 8...♘f8 (8...♕d7 9 ♗e2), when 9 ♖xh5 gxh5 10 ♕xh5 looks frightening.

b) **4...c5** 5 cxd5 ♘xd5 6 dxc5 ♘xc3 7 ♕xd8+ ♔xd8 8 bxc3 ♗g7 9 ♔d2!? ♗f5 10 f3 ♘d7 11 e4 ♗e6 12 c6 bxc6 13 ♘e2 *(82c)* (this knight has excellent prospects) 13...♗c4 14 ♔c2 ♔c7 15 h5 e5 16 ♗e3 ♗e6 17 ♘c1 a5 18 ♘b3 f5 19 ♘d2 f4 20 ♗f2 g5 21 ♗c4 ♖he8 22 ♗xe6 ♖xe6 23 ♘c4 ♗f8 24 ♖hd1. White is better and went on to win convincingly in A.Zaitsev-Smyslov, Sochi 1963.

Surprise 83   *B*

Soundness: 4   Surprise Value: 2

Nimzo-Indian: 4 ♕c2, 6...♕f5

Romanishin's idea **1 d4 ♘f6 2 c4 e6 3 ♘c3 ♗b4 4 ♕c2 d5 5 cxd5 ♕xd5 6 ♘f3 ♕f5** *(83a)*, offering a queen exchange which doubles Black's pawns, seems quite a concession, but the ending after **7 ♕xf5 exf5** does not give White serious winning chances; Black's pieces are very active, and the 'weakness' is not serious as there is no majority that White can activate to form a passed pawn. If White wants to try for a win he must keep the queens on. As **7 ♕b3 c5 8 a3 ♗xc3+ 9 ♕xc3 ♘bd7 10 g3 ♘e4 11 ♕e3 ♘df6 12 h3 0-0 13 ♗g2 ♖d8**, ½-½ Tisdall-Davies, Gausdal Eikrem mem 1997, looks very solid for Black, that leaves **7 ♕d1**, when I suggest Black plays Beliavsky's aggressive **7...e5!** *(83b)*:

a) **8 ♘xe5?** ♘e4 9 ♘d3 ♘xc3 10 ♕b3 ♘xe2+ wins a pawn, e.g. 11 ♕xb4 ♘c6.

b) **8 dxe5** ♘e4 9 ♗d2 ♘c6 10 ♘xe4 (10 e3 ♘xd2 11 ♕xd2 ♘xe5) 10...♕xe4 11 ♗xb4 (11 ♖c1 ♗g4) 11...♘xb4 12 ♖c1 ♗f5 with good counterplay.

c) **8 g4!?** and Black must choose carefully:

c1) **8...♗xc3+?!** 9 bxc3 ♘xg4 10 h3 ♘xf2 11 ♔xf2 e4 (Ig.Jelen-Beliavsky, Bled 1996) 12 ♖g1 exf3 13 e4! ♕xe4 14 ♗b5+ ♔f8 15 ♗a3+ ♔g8 16 ♕d2 gives White a powerful attack – Jelen.

c2) **8...♘xg4!** 9 ♕a4+ ♘c6 10 d5 ♗d7! (10...e4?! 11 dxc6 ♗xc3+ 12 bxc3 b5 13 ♕d4) 11 dxc6 ♗xc3+ 12 bxc3 ♗xc6 *(83c)* with fantastic counterplay, e.g. 13 ♕d1 (13 ♕b4 ♗xf3 14 exf3 ♕xf3) 13...♖d8 14 ♗d2 e4 15 h3 ♘xf2! 16 ♔xf2 exf3 17 e3 ♕d7 and White's position falls apart.

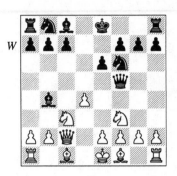

83a: after 6...♕f5

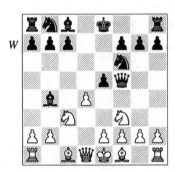

83b: after 7...e5

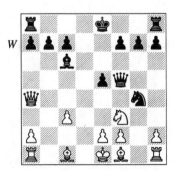

83c: after 12...♗xc6

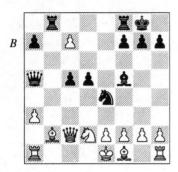

84a: after 16 c7

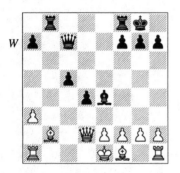

84b: after 18...d4

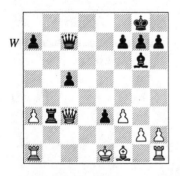

84c: after 23...☐b3

Surprise 84   B

Soundness: 3   Surprise Value: 3

Nimzo-Indian: a sharp line

The position after **1 d4 ♘f6 2 c4 e6 3 ♘c3 ♗b4 4 ♕c2 d5 5 a3 ♗xc3+ 6 ♕xc3 ♘e4 7 ♕c2 c5 8 dxc5 ♘c6 9 cxd5 exd5 10 ♘f3 ♗f5 11 b4 0-0 12 ♗b2 b6 13 b5 bxc5 14 bxc6 ♕a5+ 15 ♘d2 ☐ab8 16 c7** *(84a)* is a sharp and important one for this line of the Nimzo-Indian. Now:

a) **16...☐b3** is not considered adequate by theory: 17 ♗e5! (or 17 ☐d1 c4 18 e3 ♘g3 19 ♕xb3 cxb3 20 hxg3 ♗c2 21 ☐c1 d4 22 ♗d3 +– Kasparov-Renet, Evry simul 1989) 17...c4 18 f3 ♘xd2? (18...♘g3! is a better try) 19 ♕xd2 c3 20 ♕g5 c2+ 21 ♔f2 ♕c5+ 22 e3 ♗g6 23 ♗a6! +– M.Gurevich-Franzoni, Lucerne Wcht 1989.

b) **16...♕xc7!** (this was also condemned until very recently) **17 ♘xe4 ♗xe4 18 ♕d2 d4** *(84b)* **19 f3?!** (Rogers suggested 19 h4 afterwards) **19...♗g6 20 e4 dxe3 21 ♕c3 ☐xb2!** (21...f6? 22 ♗c4+ ♔h8 23 0-0, with a big advantage for White, was the old theoretical continuation) **22 ♕xb2 ☐b8!** (this is a move Fritz finds far more quickly than most humans; 22...♕a5+? is inadequate after 23 ♔e2 ☐e8 24 ☐c1!, e.g. 24...♕a6+ 25 ♔e1 e2 26 ♗xe2 ♗d3 27 ☐c2) and now:

b1) **23 ♕c3?** ☐b3!! *(84c)* wins since 24 ♕xb3 ♕a5+ causes disaster.

b2) **23 ♕c1** ♕a5+ 24 ♔e2 ☐b3 is also terrible for White.

b3) **23 ♗b5** ♕a5+ 24 ♔f1 ☐xb5 25 ♕e5 h6?! (25...h5 is a bit more accurate) 26 ♕xe3 (I.Rogers-Ward, British League (4NCL) 1997/8) and now 26...c4 is good for Black – Rogers.

Surprise 85   W

Soundness: 3   Surprise Value: 4

Queen's Indian: 7 e4 gambit

The sharp gambit in the Queen's Indian, **1 d4 ♘f6 2 c4 e6 3 ♘f3 b6 4 a3 ♗b7 5 ♘c3 d5 6 cxd5 ♘xd5 7 e4** *(77a)*, was briefly popular in the mid-1980s following some interesting games by Ligterink and Polovodin. However, a much-publicized victory as Black by Beliavsky convinced the chess-world that the gambit was unsound, and it vanished almost completely. However, the 'refutation' is far from clearly OK for Black, and I think 7 e4 could be used to good effect once more.

After **7...♘xc3 8 bxc3 ♗xe4** (Black must accept; otherwise White has gained a whole move over normal lines in which he plays e3 followed by e4, or misplaces his queen on c2 to force through e2-e4; however, one can expect plenty of odd deviations at move 7 and 8 at club level!) **9 ♘e5** *(77b)* Black has several possibilities:

a) **9...♗d6** 10 ♕g4 ♗g6 11 ♗b5+ forces 11...♔f8, when White has good long-term attacking prospects.

b) **9...♗e7** 10 ♕g4 ♗g6 11 ♗b5+ is similar.

c) **9...g6** 10 ♕g4 (10 h4!?) 10...♗d5 11 ♗b5+ c6 12 ♗d3 ♗g7 13 ♗g5 f6 14 c4 ♗xg2 (14...fxg5 15 cxd5 ♕xd5 16 ♗c4 ♕d6 17 0-0) 15 ♕xe6+ ♕e7 16 ♕c8+ ½-½ Graf-Sosonko, Lugano 1985.

d) **9...c6** 10 ♕e2 (10 ♕h5!?) 10...♗g6 11 h4 ♕d5 (11...f6 12 ♘xg6 hxg6 13 ♕xe6+ ♕e7 14 ♕xe7+ ♗xe7 15 g3 ± Barlov-Vučinić, Yugoslav Ch (Novi Sad) 1985) 12 ♖h3!?.

e) **9...♘d7** 10 ♗b5 c6 11 ♘xc6 ♗xc6 12 ♗xc6 ♖c8 *(85c)* 13 d5! (13 ♗b5 ♗d6 14

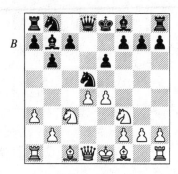

85a: after 7 e4

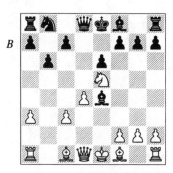

85b: after 9 ♘e5

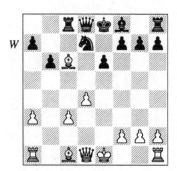

85c: after 12...♖c8

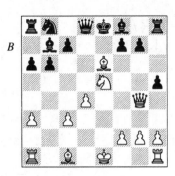

85d: after 12 ♗xe6

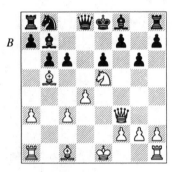

85e: after 12 ♕f3

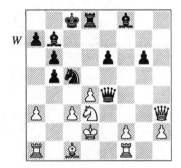

85f: after 19...♘c5

♕g4 0-0, Polovodin-Makarychev, Tallinn 1983, 15 ♗d2!?) 13...♗e7 14 ♕a4 ♕c7 15 0-0 ± S.Ivanov-Kuporosov, USSR 1984.

f) **9...a6** 10 ♕g4 ♗b7 (10...♗d5 11 ♗g5 f6 12 ♗h4 ±) 11 ♗c4 (threatening ♘xf7!) 11...h5 (11...♗d5 12 ♗g5 f6 13 ♕h5+ ± Hartoch-Van der Vliet, Amsterdam 1984) 12 ♗xe6!!? *(85d)* 12...hxg4 13 ♗xf7+ ♔e7 14 ♗g5+ ♔d6 15 ♗xd8 ♘c6 (15...♗xg2) 16 ♘c4+ ♔d7 17 ♗g5 b5 18 ♘e3 +– Ligterink-Trepp, Amsterdam 1984.

g) **9...♗b7 10 ♕h5** (10 ♗b5+ c6 11 ♕f3 ♕f6 holds) **10...g6 11 ♗b5+ c6 12 ♕f3** *(85e)* and then:

g1) **12...♕c7?!** 13 ♗d3 (13 ♗a4 b5 14 ♗f4 ♕e7 15 ♗g5 ♕c7 16 ♕f6 ♖g8 17 ♘xf7 ♕e7 18 ♘d8 ♕xf6 19 ♗xf6 ♘d7 20 ♘xb7 ½-½ Hartoch-Ligterink, Oxford 1984 is a funny game) 13...♗d6 (13...♗g7 14 ♗f4 ♕e7 15 ♘c4 ± Husari-Vuksanović, Iraklion 1995) 14 ♕f6 ♖g8 15 ♗g5 ♗xe5 16 dxe5 h6 17 ♗h4 g5 18 ♗g3 ♘d7 19 ♕xh6 0-0-0 20 0-0 ♘xe5 21 ♗h7 ♖h8 22 ♕g7 f6 23 ♕xf6 ♖xh7 24 ♕xe6+ ♖dd7 25 ♗xe5 +– Baumann-H.Bernard, corr 1987.

g2) **12...f6** 13 ♘d3 ♕d5!? (after a passive move White will have excellent play against Black's weak pawns; 13...cxb5 14 ♕xb7 ♕d5 15 ♕xd5 exd5 16 ♘f4 ♔f7 17 ♘xd5 ± Polovodin-Kaplun, USSR 1984) 14 ♕xf6 cxb5 15 ♕xh8 ♕xg2 16 ♖f1 ♕e4+ 17 ♔d2 ♘d7 18 ♕xh7 0-0-0 19 ♕h3 ♘c5! *(85f)* 20 ♘xc5 bxc5 21 ♖e1 ♗h6+ 22 ♕xh6 ♖xd4+ 23 cxd4 ♕xd4+ 24 ♔e2 ♕c4+ 25 ♔d2 ♕d4+ ½-½ A.Petrosian-Novikov, Erevan 1984.

In the variations we have just seen, White is risking little. He has good attacking possibilities, and at worst there is a forced draw or a level ending – and there are plenty of untried ideas at his disposal. In the next Surprise we look at the queen move that has all but banished 7 e4 from tournament play.

Surprise 86 W

Soundness: 3 Surprise Value: 4

The 7 e4 gambit: 9...♛h4

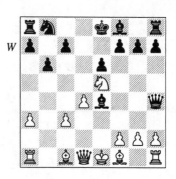

86a: after 9...♛h4

After **1 d4 ♘f6 2 c4 e6 3 ♘f3 b6 4 a3 ♗b7 5 ♘c3 d5 6 cxd5 ♘xd5 7 e4 ♘xc3 8 bxc3 ♗xe4 9 ♘e5**, the disruptive **9...♛h4** *(86a)* is the move recommended in most theory manuals. In Nogueiras-Beliavsky, Thessaloniki OL 1984, White tried 10 ♛a4+ c6 11 d5, but after 11...♗d6 12 ♘xf7 ♚xf7 13 dxe6+ ♚xe6 14 ♗e2 ♚d7 15 ♗e3 ♚c7 was a piece down for virtually nothing.

White does far better to play the obvious **10 g3**:

a) **10...♛d8** is A.Sokolov's odd idea: two tempi to provoke f3. I suggest **11 ♛a4+** c6 12 f3 ♗d5 (12...♗f5 13 ♘xc6 ♛d7 14 ♗b5) 13 c4 *(86b)* and Black can save the bishop, but his position is damaged.

b) **10...♛f6 11 ♗b5+ c6 12 f3 ♗d5** (12...♗xf3 13 ♘xf3 cxb5 14 0-0 gives White dangerous f-file play) **13 ♗e2 b5 14 a4 a6** (after 14...♗d6 15 ♘g4 ♛e7, Kallai-Stohl, Trnava 1985, I don't understand why White didn't play 16 axb5) **15 axb5 cxb5** *(86c)* and now:

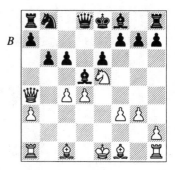

86b: after 13 c4

b1) **16 ♗f4 ♛d8 17 ♖xa6?** (spirited, but poor) 17...♖xa6 18 ♗xb5+ ♘c6 19 0-0 ♗d6 20 ♗xa6 ♗xe5 21 ♗xe5 ♘xe5 −+ Davies-Levitt, British Ch (Brighton) 1984.

b2) **16 c4 ♗b4+ 17 ♚f2 ♗b7 18 cxb5 a5 19 ♗d2 ♛e7 20 ♗xb4 ♛xb4 21 ♖a4** gave White excellent play in Bohnsack-Kohlweyer, Baden-Baden 1987, which concluded 21...♛e7 22 ♛d2 0-0 23 ♖ha1 ♖d8 24 ♖xa5 ♖xa5 25 ♖xa5 ♛d6 26 ♘c4 ♛xd4+ 27 ♛xd4 ♖xd4 28 ♖a7 ♖d7 29 ♘e5 ♖c7 30 ♘c6 ♘d7 31 ♘a5 1-0.

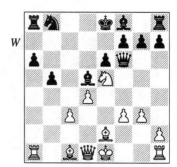

86c: after 15...cxb5

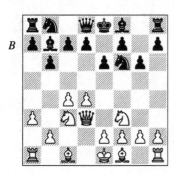

87a: after 6 ♕d3

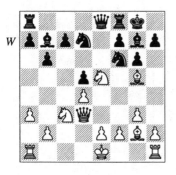

87b: after 11...♕e8

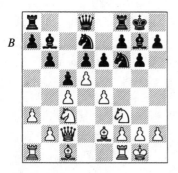

87c: after 11 d5

Surprise 87   W

Soundness: 3   Surprise Value: 2

4 a3 Queen's Indian: 5...g6

After **1 d4 ♘f6 2 c4 e6 3 ♘f3 b6 4 a3 ♗b7 5 ♘c3**, Black can try a double fianchetto with **5...g6**. This is a creative handling of the position, played many times with success by Romanishin, Korchnoi and Speelman. One idea is that if White plays d5, stifling the b7-bishop, a wonderful diagonal opens up for his colleague at g7, while 6 ♕c2, seeking to set up a big centre by 7 e4, can be met by 6...♗xf3, damaging White's pawns.

The idea we focus upon is **6 ♕d3** *(87a)*. Since the queen could now recapture on f3, Black has far more difficulty generating counterplay:

a) **6...d5** 7 cxd5 exd5 8 ♗g5 ♗g7 9 g3 0-0 10 ♗g2 ♘bd7 11 ♘e5 ♕e8 *(87b)* 12 ♘xd7 ♕xd7 13 ♗xf6 ♗xf6 14 0-0 ♗g7 15 ♖ac1 left Black with a tough defensive task in Golod-Korchnoi, Beersheba 1997.

b) **6...♗g7** 7 e4 d6 (7...d5 8 cxd5 exd5 9 e5 ♘e4 is Black's best try for activity) 8 ♗e2 0-0 9 0-0 ♘bd7 10 ♕c2 c5 (10...d5 is not feasible any more in view of 11 cxd5 exd5 12 e5 ♘e4 13 ♘xe4 dxe4 14 ♘g5) 11 d5 *(87c)* 11...e5 (11...♕e7 12 ♖e1 a6 13 ♗f1 ♘e8 14 ♗g5 ♗f6 15 ♗xf6 ♘exf6 16 ♕d2 e5 17 g3 ♖ac8 18 ♘h4 ♘h5 19 ♖ab1 ♖c7 20 ♘a4 ♖b8 21 b4 gave White a substantial plus in Oll-Romanishin, Erevan OL 1996; 11...exd5 12 exd5 affords White a pleasant space advantage) 12 g3 ♘h5 13 ♘e1 ♘df6 14 ♘g2 ♗c8 15 b4 ♕d7 16 bxc5 bxc5 17 ♖b1 ♕h3 18 ♘b5! and White is making the better progress, Karpov-Romanishin, Biel 1996.

Surprise 88   *B*

Soundness: 3   Surprise Value: 3

Bogo-Indian: a violent line

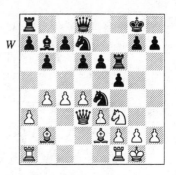

88a: after 12...♖f6

Although the Bogo is not an opening renowned for violent attacking lines, **1 d4 ♘f6 2 ♘f3 e6 3 c4 ♗b4+ 4 ♘bd2 b6 5 a3 ♗xd2+ 6 ♕xd2 ♗b7 7 e3 0-0 8 ♗e2 d6 9 0-0 ♘bd7 10 b4 ♘e4 11 ♕d3 f5 12 ♗b2** should satisfy anyone out for blood. Black's new approach here is to go directly for the white king with the minimum of subtlety: **12...♖f6** (*88a*) (rather than the older and less effective moves 12...♕f6, 12...a5, 12...♕e7, and 12...♘g5) **13 d5 ♖g6!** (again the most direct; after 13...e5? 14 ♘h4! Black is forced into 14...g6, when his rook fails to reach its target) **14 dxe6** (after 14 ♘d4 Ftačnik analysed 14...♘e5! 15 ♕c2 exd5 16 ♘xf5 dxc4 17 ♗xc4+ {17 ♗xe5 ♖xg2+!} 17...♘xc4 18 ♕xc4+ d5 19 ♕c2 ♕g5 20 ♘g3 ♘xg3 21 hxg3 c6, which is roughly equal) **14...♘f8 15 c5!** (better than 15 ♘e1 ♘xe6! 16 f3 ♕g5! 17 f4 ♕h4 18 ♕c2 ♖h6 19 ♘f3 ♕h5 20 c5 bxc5 21 ♖ad1 g5 22 h3 g4 23 ♘h2 ♕h4 24 ♘xg4 fxg4 25 ♗xg4 ♖g6 26 f5 ♖xg4 27 fxe6 ♕g3 28 ♖de1 ♘d2 0-1 Twardon-Nikolenko, Katowice 1993) **15...♘xe6 16 cxd6 cxd6 17 ♖ad1** (Dautov

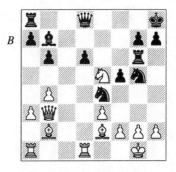

88b: after 19 ♘e5

analysed the fascinating queen sacrifice 17 ♖fd1 ♘6g5 18 ♕b3+ ♔h8 19 ♘e5 (*88b*) 19...dxe5! 20 ♖xd8+ ♖xd8 21 ♖d1 ♘d2 22 e4 f4, with attacking prospects) **17...♔h8** (*88c*) and now:

a) **18 ♕b5!** is White's best, when 18...f4! gives Black reasonable counterplay.

b) **18 ♘e1??** **♘6g5 19 ♔h1 ♘h3!** 0-1 was the shocking finish of Gelfand-Illescas, Madrid 1996.

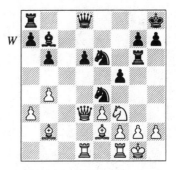

88c: after 17...♔h8

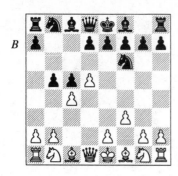

89a: after 4 f3

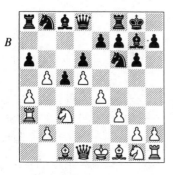

89b: after 9 ♖a3

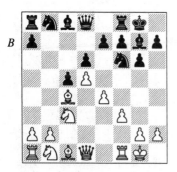

89c: after 9 ♘ec3

Surprise 89   W

Soundness: 3   Surprise Value: 3

Benko Gambit: 4 f3

After **1 d4 ♘f6 2 c4 c5 3 d5 b5, 4 f3!?** *(89a)* is a rare but interesting move. White seeks to dominate the centre, but wishes to avoid the obscurities of the line 4 cxb5 a6 5 f3 e6 (or 5...axb5). The lines are as follows:

a) **4...e6** 5 e4 exd5 (5...bxc4 6 ♘c3 exd5 7 ♘xd5 ♗b7 8 ♗xc4 ♘xd5 9 ♗xd5 gives White a firm grip, Van Vossen-Huyzer, Soest 1996) 6 cxd5 c4 7 ♘e2 ♗b7 8 ♗e3 ♘a6 9 ♘ec3 ♕a5 10 ♘d2 ♖c8 11 a4 +− Urban-Siebert, Cappelle la Grande 1997.

b) **4...g6** 5 e4 d6 6 cxb5 a6 transposes to one of Black more passive defences against 4 cxb5 a6 5 f3, viz. 5...g6 6 e4 d6. White has a few good options, e.g. 7 ♘c3 ♗g7 8 a4 0-0 9 ♖a3!? *(89b)* 9...axb5 (9...e6!? is more combative) 10 ♗xb5 ♗a6 (10...e6 11 ♘ge2 ♗b7 12 ♘f4! ±) 11 ♘ge2 ♗xb5 12 ♘xb5 ♘a6 13 0-0 ♘c7 14 ♘ec3 ♘d7 15 ♔h1 ♘b6 16 b3 with a pleasant plus, Anand-Adams, Roquebrune Amber rpd 1992.

c) **4...bxc4** 5 e4 d6 is the critical line. It seems that White's *king's* knight should head for c3, while the other knight should develop via a3. 6 ♗xc4 g6 7 ♘e2 ♗g7 8 0-0 0-0 9 ♘ec3 *(89c)* 9...♗a6 (9...♘bd7 10 a4 ♘e5 11 ♗e2 c4 12 ♗e3 e6 13 ♘a3 {13 f4!?} 13...exd5 14 exd5 ♖e8 15 ♕d2 ♗a6 ½-½ Urban-Shilov, Koszalin 1997, but 16 b4 looks good for White) 10 ♘a3 ♘fd7 11 ♗g5 h6 12 ♗h4 ♘b6 13 ♗xa6 ♘xa6 14 ♕e2 ♘b4 15 ♖ad1 ♖c8 16 f4 c4 17 e5 ♕d7 18 e6 fxe6 19 dxe6 ♕e8 20 ♗f2 ♕c6 21 ♘ab5 ♕b7 22 ♗d4 ♘d3 23 ♕g4 ♔h7 24 f5 with a strong attack, Krudde-Polgar, 1990.

Surprise 90   *W*

Soundness: 2 Surprise Value: 4

Nescafé Frappé Attack

This odd (and oddly named) line of the Benko runs **1 d4 ᐁf6 2 c4 c5 3 d5 b5 4 cxb5 a6 5 ᐁc3 axb5 6 e4 b4 7 ᐁb5 d6** (not 7...ᐁxe4? 8 ♕e2) **8 ♗c4** *(90a)*. I did a lot of work on it in the 1980s, and my games with it helped give me a reputation as a violent attacking player. I even wrote a small book on it, but a decade on, it is still very dangerous and little-known. Database searches show that several people around the world have continued to develop the NFA; we shall look at some of their ideas now. The main moves, 8...g6 and 8...ᐁbd7, are covered in the next two Surprises. Here are some rarer moves:

a) **8...ᐁxe4? 9 ♕e2** and then:

a1) **9...ᐁf6 10 ♗f4 ♖a6 11 ᐁxd6+** *(90b)* (in Liardet-Arbakov, Biel 1995, White played 11 ᐁf3?! and still beat his GM opponent) 11...♖xd6 12 ♗b5+ ♖d7 13 ♗xb8 ᐁxd5 14 0-0-0 +− was Haik-Fraguela, Lanzarote 1976. I once caught Anand with this in a blitz game, so I reckon it must be easy to miss.

a2) **9...f5 10 f3 ᐁf6 11 ♗f4 ♖a6 12 ᐁh3** g6 13 0-0 ♗g7 14 ♖fe1 h6 15 ♖ad1 ♔f7 16 ♗c1 ♖e8 17 ᐁf4 ♖b6 18 ᐁa7 ♖b7 19 ᐁxc8 ♕xc8 20 ᐁe6 ± Zhuravlev-Grushko, Kaliningrad 1976.

b) **8...♖a5 9 a4 bxa3** (9...g6 10 e5 dxe5 11 ♗e3 ♕b6 12 ♕b3 ᐁa6 13 ᐁf3 ᐁg4 14 d6 e6 15 ♖d1 ♗d7 16 ♗g5 h6 17 ♗h4 g5 18 ♗g3 ♗g7 19 h3 led to a nice win in Burgess-Simons, Keynsham rpd 1987) 10 ♖xa3 g6?! (10...♖xa3) 11 ♖xa5 ♕xa5+ 12 ♗d2 ♕d8 13 ♕a4 ♗d7 *(90c)* (Burgess-Fedorowicz, Uppingham 1988) 14 ♕a8! +−.

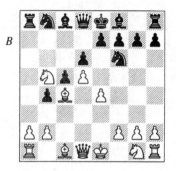

90a: after 8 ♗c4

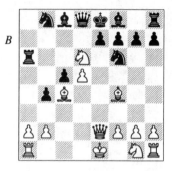

90b: after 11 ᐁxd6+

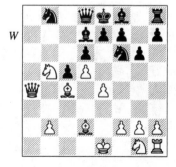

90c: after 13...♗d7

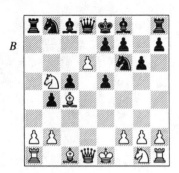

91a: after 10 d6

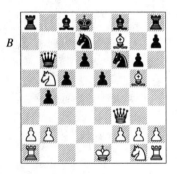

91b: after 14 ♕f3

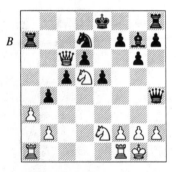

91c: after 21 a3

Surprise 91   W

Soundness: 3   Surprise Value: 4

NFA: The chaotic 8...g6

Black's most natural reply to **1 d4 ♘f6 2 c4 c5 3 d5 b5 4 cxb5 a6 5 ♘c3 axb5 6 e4 b4 7 ♘b5 d6 8 ♗c4** is **8...g6**, but at the same time it is an exceptionally risky move, since White now plays the double pawn sacrifice **9 e5 dxe5 10 d6** *(91a)*.

a) **10...♘a6** 11 ♘f3! exd6 (11...♗g7 12 ♘xe5 0-0 13 ♘c6 ♕d7 14 ♘xe7+ ♔h8 15 ♘xc8 ♖fxc8 16 0-0 ± Mensch-Capit, French Cht 1996) 12 ♗g5 is very difficult for Black, e.g. 12...♗b7 13 ♘xe5 ♕e7 14 ♘xd6+ ♕xd6 15 ♗xf7+ ♔e7 16 ♕xd6+ ♔xd6 17 ♗xf6 +− Drkulec-S.Andrews, USA 1992.

b) **10...exd6 11 ♗g5** and then:

b1) **11...♘bd7!?** 12 ♕b3 ♕b6 (better than 12...♘b6?! 13 ♗xf7+ ♔e7 14 ♖d1 c4 15 ♗xc4 ♘xc4 16 ♕xc4 ♗e6 17 ♕h4 ♔f7 18 ♘f3 +− Fang-Palatnik, Philadelphia 1994) 13 ♗xf7+ ♔d8 14 ♕f3 *(91b)* 14...d5 15 ♕xd5 ♗b7 16 ♗xf6+ ♗e7 17 ♗xe7+ ♔xe7 18 ♕c4 ♗a6 19 ♗d5 ♖af8 20 ♕h4+ ♖f6 21 ♗c4 ♗xb5 22 ♘f3 ± Labarthe-Liardet, Geneva 1992.

b2) **11...♗b7** 12 ♗d5!? ♗xd5 (Black probably has to sacrifice his queen by 12...♘xd5 13 ♗xd8 ♔xd8, but it's unconvincing) 13 ♗xf6 ♕xf6 14 ♕xd5 ♖a4 15 ♘c7+ ♔d8 16 ♕b7 ♘d7 17 ♘d5 ♕h4 18 ♘e2 ♔e8 19 0-0! ♗g7 20 ♕c6 ♖a7 21 a3! *(91c)* 1-0 Hergert-Leisebein, corr 1996.

b3) **11...♖a5** (the 'main line') **12 ♘f3 h6** (12...♗g4 13 ♕b3 ±; 12...♘c6 13 ♘d2! ±) 13 ♘xe5 hxg5 14 ♘xf7 ♕e7+ 15 ♔f1 ♖xb5 16 ♘xh8 is wildly unclear.

Surprise 92   *W*

Soundness: 3 Surprise Value: 4

NFA: The solid 8...♘bd7

After **1 d4 ♘f6 2 c4 c5 3 d5 b5 4 cxb5 a6 5 ♘c3 axb5 6 e4 b4 7 ♘b5 d6 8 ♗c4 ♘bd7** White must be very precise not to allow a trick. Following **9 ♘f3** *(92a)* Black can try:

a) **9...g6** 10 e5 ♘xe5 11 ♘xe5 dxe5 12 d6 exd6 13 ♗g5 ♖b8 (13...♖a5?! 14 ♕f3 ♗g7 15 ♕c6+ ♔e7 16 0-0-0 +– S.Smith-P.Wason, corr 1994) 14 ♕b3!? h6 15 ♗xf7+ ♔e7 16 ♘a7 ♕c7 17 ♗xg6 ♗e6 18 ♕f3 ± Ed.David-Shantharam, Gausdal 1991.

b) **9...♘b6 10 ♗d3 g6** (10...♖a5 11 a4 ♗d7 12 ♘d2 g6 13 b3 ♗g7 14 ♗b2 0-0 15 0-0 ♘g4 16 ♗xg7 ♔xg7 17 ♖e1 ♘e5 18 ♗f1 g5 19 ♘f3 f6 20 ♘xe5 fxe5 21 ♕d2 h6 22 ♘a3 ♖f4 23 ♘c2 ± Burgess-Katišonok, Võsu 1989; 10...c4 11 ♗xc4! ♘xc4 12 ♕c2!) **11 b3 ♗g7 12 ♗b2 0-0 13 0-0** *(92b)*:

b1) **13...e6** (played by Fedorowicz) 14 ♕c2! exd5 15 ♘xd6!.

b2) **13...♖a5** 14 a4 bxa3 15 ♖xa3 ♖xa3 16 ♘xa3 ♗d7 17 ♕d2 ♕c7 18 ♘c4 ♖a8 19 ♗c3 ♘xc4?! 20 bxc4 ♖a4 21 e5 ♘e8 22 ♖e1 ♕a7 23 h4 ± Burgess-Beaumont, Hanham 1988.

b3) **13...♗a6** 14 a4! (14 ♖e1 =; 14 ♕e2? ♕d7 15 a4 bxa3 16 ♖xa3 ♘h5 17 ♗xg7 ♔xg7 18 g3 ♘f4 ∓ Burgess-Beaumont, Århus 1990) 14...bxa3 15 ♘xa3 ♕d7 16 h3 ♖fb8 17 ♖e1 ♕b7 18 ♗c2 ♖d8 19 ♖a2 ♖d7 20 ♘d2 ♕c8 21 ♗c3 ♕f8 22 ♖a1 ♖dd8 23 ♘ab1 *(92c)* (impressive manoeuvring; White is now ready for action) 23...♗b7 24 ♖a7 ♖d7 25 ♕a5 ♖xa7 26 ♕xa7 ♘c8 27 ♕a4 ♕d8 28 ♗a5 ♕f8 29 ♗d3 e6 30 dxe6 fxe6 31 ♗c4 ± Mensch-Pinski, Budapest 1997.

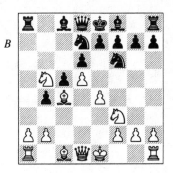

92a: after 9 ♘f3

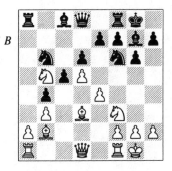

92b: after 13 0-0

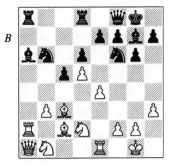

92c: after 23 ♘ab1

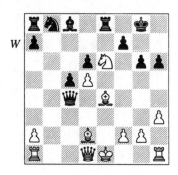

93a: after 16...♕c4

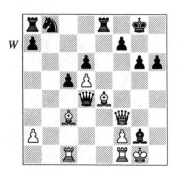

93b: after 20...♗xg2

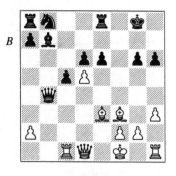

93c: after 20 ♔f1

Surprise 93   *B*

Soundness: 2   Surprise Value: 4

♗d3 Benoni – a try for Black

The system against the Modern Benoni based on ♘f3, h3, e4 and ♗d3 is extremely annoying for Black. Here is an attempt to revive Black's fortunes. It's risky, but it might just work. Failing that, it might work once or twice!

After **1 d4 ♘f6 2 c4 c5 3 d5 e6 4 ♘c3 exd5 5 cxd5 d6 6 e4 g6 7 h3 ♗g7 8 ♘f3 0-0 9 ♗d3**, I propose that Black try **9...b5** and then after **10 ♘xb5** play the 'refuted' move **10...♘xe4** (the main line, 10...♖e8 is under considerable pressure). Assuming White knows his stuff, you will get the following moves: **11 ♗xe4 ♖e8 12 ♘g5 h6 13 ♘e6 ♕a5+ 14 ♘c3 ♗xc3+ 15 bxc3 ♕xc3+ 16 ♗d2 ♕c4** *(93a)*.

a) The official refutation continues **17 ♕f3 ♗xe6 18 ♖c1 ♕d4 19 0-0 ♗xh3 20 ♗c3** and now Black is supposed to lose after 20...♕xe4 21 ♖ce1. However, 20...♗xg2!! *(93b)* seems OK for Black: 21 ♕xg2? ♕xe4; 21 ♔xg2? ♕xe4; 21 ♗xd4? ♗xf3; 21 ♕f4 ♕xe4 22 ♖ce1 (22 ♕f6? ♖e5 23 ♖fe1 ♕g4 gives Black a decisive counterattack; 22 ♕xh6? ♖e5 23 ♖fe1 ♕g4 is similar) 22...♘d7 23 ♕xh6 f6 looks unclear, e.g. 24 ♖xe4 ♗xe4 25 ♕f4 (25 ♖e1?! ♗f5) 25...♗xd5 26 ♖d1 (26 ♕xd6 ♗e6 27 ♖e1 ♗f5) 26...♗e6.

b) **17 ♗f3 fxe6 18 ♗e3 ♗b7 19 ♖c1 ♕b4+ 20 ♔f1** *(93c)* (my recommendation in *Beating the Indian Defences*) offers White compensation, but is not too clear. Yes, I'd rather be White, but all is not lost for Black, after, say, 20...♘d7!?.

Surprise 94 *B*

Soundness: 3   Surprise Value: 3

Fajarowicz: 4 a3 b6

In case you weren't sure, the Fajarowicz is an off-shoot of the Budapest Defence, with Black, after **1 d4 ♘f6 2 c4 e5 3 dxe5**, playing the uncompromising **3...♘e4**. This stands up well against most replies thanks to Black's piece-play with ...♗b4(+) and in some cases a ...d5 pawn sacrifice. However, Black has never found a convincing answer to **4 a3**, preventing the bishop check, and preparing to return the pawn in such lines as 4...♘c6 5 ♘f3 d6 6 ♕c2! ♘c5 7 b4 ♘e6 8 ♗b2 dxe5 9 e3! for heavy positional pressure. **4...b6!?** *(94a)* might solve Black's problems:

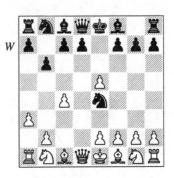

94a: after 4...b6

a) **5 g3 ♗b7 6 ♗g2?** looks natural, but then Black has the trick 6...♘c3.

b) **5 ♘d2 ♗b7 6 ♕c2 ♘xd2 7 ♗xd2 a5 8 f3 ♗c5!** *(94b)* 9 e4 ♘c6 10 ♗c3 ♕e7 (10...♕g5!?) 11 ♘e2 (11 f4!?) 11...♘xe5 12 ♘d4 f6 13 ♘f5 ♕f7 14 ♕d2 a4 15 ♗d4 ♘c6 16 ♗xc5 bxc5 17 ♗d3 g6 18 ♘e3 ♘d4 gave Black an attractive position in Timoshchenko-G.Welling, Ostend 1991.

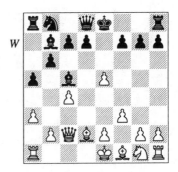

94b: after 8...♗c5

c) **5 ♘f3 ♗b7** and then:

c1) **6 e3 ♘c6 7 b3 ♕e7 8 ♗b2 0-0-0 9 ♕c2 ♘g5!** *(94c)* (an important manoeuvre) 10 ♗e2 ♘xf3+ 11 ♗xf3 ♘xe5 12 ♗xb7+ ♔xb7 13 ♘c3 ♕e6 14 ♕e4+ c6 15 ♘e2 ♘g6 16 ♕c2 ♘h4 17 0-0 ♕g6 18 ♕xg6 hxg6 with a satisfactory game for Black, Sarmiento-Romero, Mesa 1992.

c2) **6 g3 ♕e7 7 ♗g2 ♘c6 8 ♗f4 ♕c5 9 0-0 ♕xc4 10 ♘bd2 ♘xd2 11 ♕xd2** was my recommendation for White in *Beating the Indian Defences*. While I'd rather be White, Black has chances too.

94c: after 9...♘g5

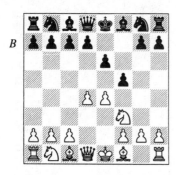

95a: after 3 e4

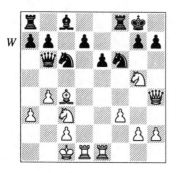

95b: after 15...♕b6

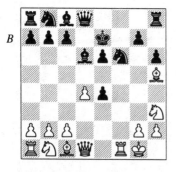

95c: after 10 0-0

Surprise 95   W

Soundness: 3   Surprise Value: 4

Dutch: Bellon Gambit

This interesting gambit arises after the moves **1 d4 e6** (this move-order is often used by those who wish to avoid such lines as 1...f5 2 ♘c3 or 2 ♗g5) **2 ♘f3 f5 3 e4** (*95a*). After **3...fxe4 4 ♘g5 ♘f6 5 f3** Black faces a choice. The main line, 5...c5 is discussed in the next Surprise. Other defences:

a) **5...exf3** 6 ♕xf3 ♘c6 7 c3 ♗e7 8 ♗d3 0-0 and now 9 0-0 gives White definite attacking chances, whereas 9 ♕h3 h6 10 ♗g6 was possibly a bit reckless in Netusil-Vavruska, Czech Cht 1993.

b) **5...e3** 6 ♗xe3 c5 7 ♘c3 cxd4 8 ♕xd4 ♘c6 9 ♕h4 ♘b4 10 0-0-0 ♕a5 11 ♗c4 ♗c5 12 ♗xc5 ♕xc5 13 ♖he1 0-0 14 a3 ♘c6 15 b4 ♕b6 (*95b*) 16 ♘d5!! exd5 17 ♖xd5 h6 18 ♖d6+ 1-0 Bellon-Garcia Fernandez, Spanish Ch (Lleida) 1991.

c) **5...h6** 6 ♘h3 d5 (6...exf3 7 ♕xf3 – compare 'a') 7 fxe4 dxe4 (7...♘xe4 8 ♕h5+ ♔d7 9 ♗d3 gives White obvious compensation) 8 ♗e2 ♗d6 9 ♗h5+ ♔e7 10 0-0 (*95c*) 10...♘c6 (10...e5 11 ♘f2 exd4 12 ♘xe4 ♘xe4 13 ♖f7+ ♔e6 14 ♕g4+ ♔d5 15 c4+ gives White a winning attack) 11 ♘c3 ♘xd4 12 ♘xe4! ♘f5 (12...♘xe4 13 ♖f7+ ♔e8 14 ♕g4) 13 ♕e2 ♘xe4?! (13...♘d4 14 ♕f2 ♖f8 15 ♘xd6 ♕xd6 16 ♘f4 gives White excellent compensation) 14 ♕xe4 ♗c5+ 15 ♔h1 ♕d5 16 ♕e1 ♗d6 17 ♘f4 ♗xf4 18 ♗xf4 ♖f8 19 ♗xc7 a5 20 ♕c3 ♖a6 21 ♕a3+ ♘d6 22 ♖fd1 ♕e5 23 ♖xd6! ♖xd6 24 ♖d1 1-0 Gretarsson-Smyslov, Reykjavik 1995.

Surprise 96   W

Soundness: 3   Surprise Value: 4

Dutch: Bellon Gambit 5...c5

After **1 d4 e6 2 ♘f3 f5 3 e4 fxe4 4 ♘g5 ♘f6
5 f3 c5!**, White replies **6 fxe4 cxd4** (Black is
happy to return the pawn to kill off White's
initiative) **7 ♗d3!** *(96a)*, making a genuine
gambit of it, when again Black must make a
decision:

a) **7...♘c6 8 0-0** and then:

a1) **8...d6 9 c3!** h6 10 ♘f3 ♗e7 11 cxd4
0-0 12 ♘c3 e5 13 ♗c4+ ♔h7 14 ♔h1 ♗g4
15 ♗e3 ± Benjamin-Machulsky, New York
Open 1990.

a2) **8...♗d6 9 ♘a3 ♗e5** *(96b)* 10 b4!?
(10 ♘c4 transposes to Bellon-Vaiser in 'b')
10...0-0 11 ♘c4 a6 12 a4 d6 13 ♗d2 ♕e8 14
♕e2 gave White pressure in Bellon-Vega
Holm, Spanish Cht 1994. Then 14...♕g6?
left White with a number of tempting options, of which the simple 15 ♘b6 ♖b8 16
♘xc8 followed by 17 ♘xe6, regaining the
pawn with a very good position, would certainly have been the clearest.

b) **7...♗d6 8 0-0 ♗e5 9 ♘d2** (perhaps
Bellon would now prefer 9 ♘a3) 9...♘c6 10
♘c4 0-0 11 c3 d6 12 ♔h1 dxc3 13 bxc3 h6
14 ♘f3 ♗xc3 15 ♖b1 *(96c)* 15...d5 16 exd5
exd5 17 ♗a3 (White's imaginative play in
this game is extremely impressive) 17...dxc4
18 ♗xc4+ ♔h8 19 ♗xf8 ♕xf8 20 ♕d3 ♗b4
21 ♘h4 ♕d6? (21...♘e5 was essential, e.g.
22 ♕g3 ♕c5 23 ♕xe5 ♕xc4 24 ♖f4 ♕xa2)
22 ♘g6+ ♔h7 23 ♘e5+ ♕xd3 24 ♗xd3+
♔g8 25 ♘xc6 led to a win for White in
Bellon-Vaiser, Helsinki 1991.

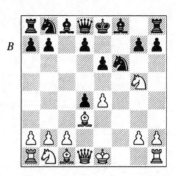

96a: after 7 ♗d3

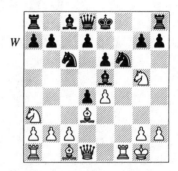

96b: after 9...♗e5

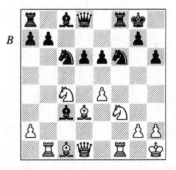

96c: after 15 ♖b1

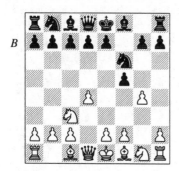

97a: after 3 g4

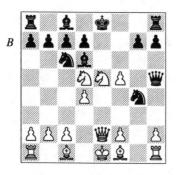

97b: after 9 ♘xe5

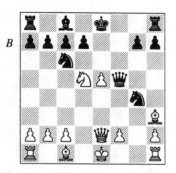

97c: after 11 ♗h3

Surprise 97   W

Soundness: 2 Surprise Value: 4

Dutch: Bogoljubow Gambit

This is an old and completely forgotten gambit idea that was tried successfully by Bogoljubow in the early part of his career.

It goes: **1 d4 f5 2 ♘c3 ♘f6** (after 2...d5 3 e4!?, Black must of course avoid 3...fxe4? 4 ♕h5+, while after 3...dxe4 White has the choice between 4 ♗g5 and 4 ♗c4 followed by ♘h3 or f3) and now **3 g4** (*97a*). Unlike some other berserk gambits with g4 against the Dutch (e.g. 2 g4?! fxg4 3 h3, when 3...g3! is a very good reply), the idea here isn't so much to break open the h-file but rather to dominate the centre. Then:

a) **3...fxg4** can be met by 4 e4 d6 5 h3.

b) **3...♘xg4 4 e4 e5** (this attempt to refute White's play is unconvincing) **5 exf5! ♕h4 6 ♕e2 ♘c6 7 ♘f3 ♕h5 8 ♘d5 ♗d6 9 ♘xe5!** (*97b*) and then:

b1) **9...♘xd4** 10 ♘xg4+ (not 10 ♕xg4? ♕xg4 11 ♘xg4 ♘xc2+) 10...♘xe2 11 ♘gf6+ gxf6 12 ♘xf6+ is Bogoljubow's analysis – White is doing well.

b2) **9...♗xe5** 10 dxe5 ♕xf5 (10...♘d4 11 ♕e4 ♘xf5 12 ♗e2 is also disastrous) 11 ♗h3! (*97c*) 11...h5 12 f3 ♕f7 13 ♘xc7+ ♔d8 14 ♘xa8 ♘d4 15 fxg4 1-0 Bogoljubow-Weindl, Stockholm 1920. There would follow 15...♘xe2 16 ♗g5+ ♔e8 17 ♘c7+ ♔f8 18 ♖f1.

So, on move 4, Black should try something like 4...d6, but White will have a good deal of play for the pawn after 5 ♗h3.

Surprise 98 *B*

Soundness: 3 Surprise Value: 3

Trompowsky: 2...e6 3 e4 c5

Here we consider an unusual reply to the popular Trompowsky, **1 d4 ♘f6 2 ♗g5**. When Black plays **2...e6**, the idea is usually to meet **3 e4** (instead 3 ♘f3 is a Torre, but in general, if White wanted a Torre, he would have played 2 ♘f3) with 3...h6, losing time to gain the bishop-pair. Instead **3...c5!?** *(98a)* is a very interesting idea that is not mentioned in *ECO*. Then:

a) **4 ♘f3** leaves White over-extended. 4...cxd4 is a good reply, while 4...♕b6 looks tempting.

b) **4 d5 ♕b6** *(98b)* is more annoying for White than the similar line 2...c5 3 ♗xf6 gxf6 4 d5 ♕b6 5 ♕c1 ♗h6 6 e3, since after 5 ♗xf6 gxf6 6 ♕c1 ♗h6 White has no adequate reply.

c) **4 e5 h6** (forced) and then:

c1) **5 ♗h4?!** g5 6 ♗g3 ♘e4! 7 c3 cxd4 8 ♕xd4 ♘xg3 9 hxg3 ♘c6 10 ♕e3 b6 11 ♗d3 ♕c7 12 f4 ♗b7 13 ♘f3 0-0-0 14 ♘bd2 d6 15 ♘xg5 dxe5 16 ♘h3 ♖g8 17 0-0-0 ♗c5 18 ♕e2 ♖xg3 19 ♘f1 ♖gg8 20 f5 ♘d4 21 cxd4 ♖xg2 22 ♘f2 ♗xd4+ 23 ♕c2 ♕xc2+ 24 ♗xc2 ♖xf2 0-1 Povah-Rowson, British League (4NCL) 1997/8. A very nice dynamic game by the young Scottish star.

c2) **5 ♗c1 ♘d5** (an improved c3 Sicilian for Black!) 6 c4 *(98c)* 6...♘b6 (6...♘b4 could be tried – compare Sherzer's idea in Surprise 22) 7 dxc5 ♗xc5 8 ♘f3 d5 9 exd6 ♕xd6 10 ♕xd6 ♗xd6 11 ♘c3 ♘c6 12 ♗d2 ♘d7 13 0-0-0 ♔e7 14 ♘b5 ½-½ Soffer-Yudasin, Israeli Ch (Tel-Aviv) 1994.

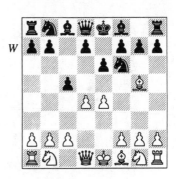

98a: after 3...c5

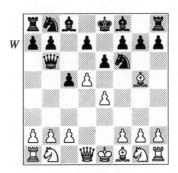

98b: after 4...♕b6

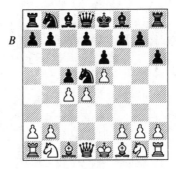

98c: after 6 c4

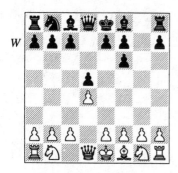

99a: after 3...gxf6

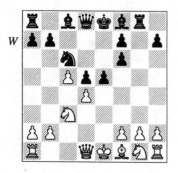

99b: after 8...e5

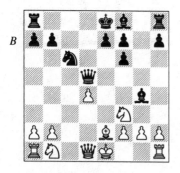

99c: after 9 ♗e2

Surprise 99   B

Soundness: 3 Surprise Value: 2

Trompowsky: 2...d5, 3...gxf6

It is possible for Black to drum up some interesting possibilities against the Trompowsky, **1 d4 ♘f6 2 ♗g5**, by playing the solid **2...d5**, provided he answers **3 ♗xf6** (3 ♘f3 ♘e4 is a very comfortable version of the Torre for Black) with **3...gxf6!?** *(99a)*. This seems to me the natural way to recapture, though it is quite rare. Black intends to get counterplay with a quick ...c5 as we see in the following variations:

a) **4 ♘c3 e6 5 e3 c5 6 ♘ge2 ♘c6 7 g3** cxd4 8 exd4 h5 9 ♗g2 h4 with counterplay, Aleksandrov-Tunik, Voskresensk 1993.

b) **4 c4 c5 5 ♘c3 cxd4 6 ♕xd4 dxc4 7 ♕xd8+ ♔xd8 8 e4 e6 9 ♗xc4 ♗b4 10 ♘ge2 ♗d7** is very solid for Black, Meduna-Balashov, Trnava 1988.

c) **4 e3 c5 5 c4 cxd4** and then:

c1) **6 ♕xd4** and here, rather than 6...dxc4 7 ♕xd8+ ♔xd8 8 ♗xc4 ±, 6...♗e6 looks quite OK, while 6...♘c6 (riskier) 7 ♕xd5 ♕xd5 8 cxd5 ♘b4 9 ♘a3 ♘xd5 might hang together too.

c2) **6 exd4 ♘c6** and here:

c21) **7 c5?! ♖g8 8 ♘c3 e5!?** *(99b)* **9 ♗b5 ♖xg2 10 ♕f3 ♖g6 11 ♕xd5 exd4 12 ♗xc6+ bxc6 13 ♕xc6+ ♗d7** and Black won quickly, T.Wall-Sadler, British Ch (Nottingham) 1996.

c22) **7 cxd5 ♕xd5 8 ♘f3 ♗g4** (8...e5!? 9 ♘c3 ♗b4 10 ♕d2 ♗xc3 11 bxc3 exd4 12 cxd4 ♖g8 is OK for Black, San Segundo-Andersson, Pamplona 1997/8) **9 ♗e2** *(99c)* and now I see no reason why Black can't get away with 9...♗xf3 10 ♗xf3 ♕e6+, e.g. 11 ♔f1 ♕c4+ 12 ♔g1 ♘xd4.

Surprise 100   *W*

Soundness: 4 Surprise Value: 3

Schmid Benoni 5...0-0 6 e5!

The position after **1 d4 ♘f6 2 ♘f3 c5 3 d5 g6 4 ♘c3 ♗g7 5 e4** can arise from various move-orders (1 e4 c5 2 ♘f3 g6 3 d4 ♗g7 4 d5 ♘f6 5 ♘c3 being another) and here the move Black would like to play is **5...0-0**. The point is that Black would like to do without the move ...d6, not just to cut out ♗b5+, but also to make some tricks like 6 ♗e2?! b5! 7 ♗xb5 ♘xe4 work. However, White has the powerful reply **6 e5!** *(100a)*.

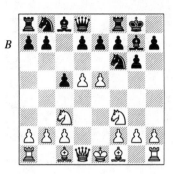

100a: after 6 e5

Then 6...♘e8?! 7 h4! d6 8 e6! fxe6 9 h5 gave White a powerful attack in Yermolinsky-Khmelnitsky, USA Ch (Modesto) 1995. Yermolinsky's main idea is that the natural **6...♘g4** is answered by the stunning novelty **7 ♘g5!** (7 ♗f4?! is feeble by comparison):

a) **7...♘xe5** 8 f4 f6 (8...h6 9 ♘h3 traps the knight) 9 ♘xh7! *(100b)* 9...♔xh7 10 fxe5 fxe5 11 ♗d3 with an enormous attack.

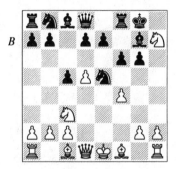

100b: after 9 ♘xh7

b) **7...d6** 8 e6 ♘xf2 will give Black a few pawns for the piece, but is unconvincing.

c) **7...h5** is Baburin's suggestion, and probably Black's only hope.

d) **7...♘h6** 8 h4 f6 (8...♗xe5 9 h5 ♘f5 10 ♘xh7!! gives White a winning attack) 9 ♘ge4! ♘f7 (9...fxe5 10 h5) 10 h5! f5 11 ♘g5 *(100c)* 11...♘xg5 (11...♗xe5 12 ♘xh7!) 12 ♗xg5 ♗xe5 (12...h6 13 hxg6! hxg5 14 ♖h8+!!) 13 hxg6 hxg6 14 d6! ♗f6 15 ♗xf6 ♖xf6 16 ♗c4+ e6 17 ♕d2 ♕f8 (17...♖f7 puts up more resistance) 18 ♘d5! exd5 19 ♗xd5+ ♖e6+ 20 ♗xe6+ dxe6 21 ♕g5 ♗d7 22 0-0-0 ♗e8 23 ♕d8! 1-0 Khuzman-Minasian, Pula Echt 1997.

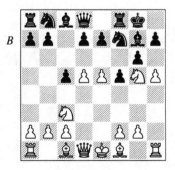

100c: after 11 ♘g5

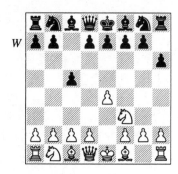

101a: after 2...h6

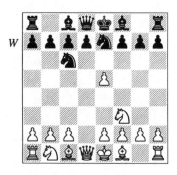

101b: after 3...♘ge7

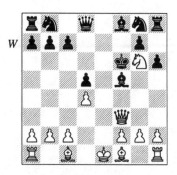

101c: after 10...♗f5

Surprise 101

Soundness: ? Surprise Value: ?

And finally...

Here are three ideas that didn't quite justify a full page in the book...

Sicilian: Bücker's 2...h6
By playing **1 e4 c5 2 ♘f3 h6** *(101a)*, Black intends 3 d4 cxd4 4 ♘xd4 ♘f6 5 ♘c3 e5, when after 6 ♘db5 d6, he gets a Pelikan-type position where White cannot play ♗g5. However, cute though that idea is, if White plays some other third move (e.g. 3 c3) it is hard to see Black justifying ...h6.

Zilbermints Gambit
This arises after **1 d4 e5 2 dxe5 ♘c6 3 ♘f3 ♘ge7** *(101b)*, and is possibly the best attempt to make 1...e5 viable. That, however, may not be saying very much. I find Black's position hard to believe after either 4 ♗g5 h6 5 ♗h4 g5 6 ♗g3 or 4 ♘c3 ♘g6 5 ♗g5 ♗e7 6 ♗xe7 ♘gxe7, but maybe I should have more faith...

The Original Philidor
Although the Russian player Maliutin has revived this ancient line, **1 e4 e5 2 ♘f3 d6 3 d4 f5**, with success and, for instance actually won a game from the position after 4 ♘c3 fxe4 5 ♘xe4 d5 6 ♘eg5 h6 7 ♘f7 ♔xf7 8 ♘xe5+ ♔e7 9 ♘g6+ ♔f6 10 ♕f3+ ♗f5 *(101c)* 11 ♘xh8 ♕e7+ 12 ♗e2 ♕e4 13 g4 ♕xf3 14 ♗xf3 ♗xc2 15 h4 ♘c6 16 g5+ ♔f5, I think we can leave this as his exclusive domain!